Real Life
Moments

A Dad's Devotional

J. Mark Fox

Real Life Moments
A Dad's Devotional
by J. Mark Fox

Antioch Community Church
1600 Powerline Rd.
Elon, NC 27244
(336) 586-0997
markfox@antiochchurch.cc
www.antiochchurch.cc

First published by Dog Ear Publishing
4010 W. 86th Street, Ste H
Indianapolis, IN 46268
www.dogearpublishing.net

dog ear
PUBLISHING

ISBN: 978-159858-557-5

This book is printed on acid-free paper.

Printed in the United States of America

I dedicate this book to all the Dads I know
who are bringing up their sons and daughters
in the training and admonition of the Lord.

Foreword

One of the most challenging things I have faced as the husband of one wife and the father of five boys and two girls is the same thing you have faced, no matter how many children you have. It is a constant challenge to be the husband and the father we are called by God to be and to give our wife and children what they need us to give. All along the way, I have looked for examples of other men who desire to be godly leaders. I have read their books and listened to their stories, gleaning from their successes and their failures.

This book is designed to be read by the dad who is busy making a living at a job but does not want to overlook making a life at home. My hope is that each story will make you laugh or think or even cry, and that God will use this book to encourage you in your own journey as a godly man.

There are fifty-two life lessons in this book, one for each week of the year. They are not dated, so you can start anytime in the year and use it for the next 52 weeks. Or, you can read the lessons in 52 days if you like. Or, 52 hours. Hey, you could probably read through the whole book in about 52 minutes, but I don't think you would be able to do all the "action" items that fast. Nor would you want to!

At the end of each lesson, there is a prayer you can read as an encouragement to your own heart's cry to the Lord.

There is also an action item that exhorts you to <u>do</u> something in response to what you just read. Hey, I'm a guy, too. I know the tendency we guys have to believe that just *thinking* about something, or just *hearing* a good idea and agreeing with it is equivalent to actually *DOING* it! Sorry. I wish it were so, but that's just not going to fly. Go ahead and check your bags with Reality Airlines and follow through on those good intentions you have entertained for years. This book, I hope, will help you to do that.

If nothing else, you will have a collection of wild and funny and sobering stories to share with your family around the supper table. Or, if you are a pastor or a teacher, these pages can help you illustrate biblical truths in your next sermon or Sunday School lesson.

No matter how you use this book, my prayer is that it will be a blessing to you. And I would love to hear from you. Feel free to email me at markfox@antiochchurch.cc You can visit the church website at www.antiochchurch.cc I look forward to it!

Blessings,

J. Mark Fox

A glad father enjoys the fruit of his labor

"A wise son makes a glad father,
but a foolish son is the grief of his mother."
(Proverbs 10:1)

Recently I had the opportunity to spend the better part of an afternoon with a good friend of mine. I was flying to Kenya and had a six-hour layover in Detroit. So, my friend came and picked me up at the airport, we found a little cafe close by, and had a pleasant lunch together. Then we asked directions to the nearest Starbucks, and spent another two hours there, enjoying the fact that neither one of us had to be anywhere that afternoon, there was nothing pressing us, and we could simply enjoy the company, the wonderful smell of coffee brewing, and the laughter of good friends.

We talked easily of old times, swapped stories, joked around, and just enjoyed being together. I reflected later on the plane how much I love this friend of mine, and look forward to the next time we can be together. The funny thing is, though we have known each other for 21 years, our relationship has changed drastically in the last two.

You see, this friend is also my oldest son. Micah attends college about an hour from Detroit, and was able to come down and hang out with his Dad for half a day. We talked about the courses he is taking in college and the things he is learning about life. We discussed the job offer he has waiting for him after he graduates this May. We laughed about college pranks, and we agonized together about our favorite NFL team's loss in the playoffs. We talked about theology and about career choices and about marriage.

When Micah dropped me off at the airport and we hugged, it felt as natural and as easy to say "I love you" to my son as anything I have ever done.

What a blessing! I felt like I was sitting down to a banquet of fresh fruits and vegetables that my wife and I had planted in a different season. All of the agony of back-breaking toil in the hot sun was forgotten because the harvest was in and the feast was prepared. The labor was eclipsed by the sweet reward. The fruit was delicious and satisfying.

I am not writing this to point to myself as a good father. Believe me when I say that I have made as many mistakes as anyone. I remember a basketball game that almost came to blows because of my own pride and stubborn competitiveness. Micah's cooler head prevailed and we were spared what could have been a devastating blow to our relationship. I remember many times when I disciplined in anger. I remember several years of awkward embarrassment between us as he grew into manhood and the hugs were fewer than they should have been, the expressions of love forced at times, absent at others. I remember the times I didn't do the thing my son needed and the times I did or said the wrong thing. But I am eternally grateful and I give praise to the one who is able to take my meager efforts and my mistakes and redeem them for his own glorious purposes. He has certainly done that in my relationship with Micah. And I trust God will do the same with each of my children.

A wise son makes a glad father? Then this is one glad dad.

❧

Prayer: "Lord, help me not to grow weary in the planting season, so that You and I can enjoy the harvest!"

Action: What can you do with your children today to let them know you love them? Something as simple as a game of whiffleball in the backyard can be a building block to stronger relationships with our children.

You can, in fact, come home again

But Jesus said to them,
"A prophet is not without honor except in his own country
and in his own house."
(Matthew 13:57)

It was an invitation that took me by surprise. The last time I preached in my home church, the one I grew up in, was in 1986. So, to get an invitation 20 years later to come and share with the folks there was exciting. It was a rare opportunity for a local boy who was known by many in the congregation as "a handful." That was one of the nicer phrases used to describe this middle of three boys who always seemed to be getting into some trouble or the other.

I remember the Sunday evening when I was sitting near the back of the sanctuary with a lot of my teenage buddies. We were having a big old time snickering, passing notes to one another, whispering jokes down the line, and basically making nuisances of ourselves. The man in the pew in front of us began to turn red. It started at the base of his neck and worked its way up, out onto both ears, and continued up to the top of his head. Then he started to shake. Just a little at first, and it looked like he was stifling a laugh, but I could tell that wasn't it. He had one hand stretched out to the right and as he gripped the pew to keep from shaking, his knuckles turned white. My eyes bounced from his white-knuckled death-grip on the pew to his neck that was beet red to his shoulders shaking with adrenalin. When the tremors grew worse and it looked like he was about to blow, I stared in fascination at what I knew was about to occur. He finally couldn't take it any more. His southern gentility broke like a dam and he turned and faced us with a fury. In a stage whisper that half the church could hear, he told us that this was the house of God and that we were interrupting the service and that if we could not sit still and be quiet and listen, we should just get up and leave! He was right, of course, but we were too smart to know it at the time. I had the sense as a 15-year-old that is common to that species, the sense that I knew just about everything there was to know. The only thing I didn't understand was why older people were so dense. Like I said, I was "a handful."

Flash ahead nearly 35 years and here I am, back in my home church. Only this time I am not sitting in the back making a disturbance. I am in the front, watching my children. We had been invited to come and share about the mission trip to Kenya that seven of us from Antioch took this summer. Two of the seven were Caleb and Hannah. I sat and fought the tears as I heard my 19-year-old share how God has changed his heart each time he has traveled to Kenya with me. I nearly fell apart as I listened to my 17-year-old tell how God used the trip to challenge her thinking and deepen her love for the Father. The other team members shared testimonies and songs and my heart was overflowing with gratitude at what God has done in my life in spite of me.

It is hard to get a hearing at home, sometimes. But you can go home again. You can.

✤

Prayer: "Lord, give my children (and me) a vision for the world."

Action: Plan a mission trip with at least one of your children. It doesn't have to be across the sea; it could be across town at the homeless shelter!

As dads, we only get one chance

*"Seek first the kingdom of God and His righteousness,
and all these things shall be added to you."*
(Matthew 6:33)

A woman in Chicago in the late 1800s entreated her husband to go with her to hear DL Moody preach. "I'm going to the bar," he replied. He walked into the winter cold of the Windy City to make his way to a favorite watering hole. It wasn't long before he heard a "crunch, crunch" behind him and he was surprised to see his little son trying to catch up.

"Where are you going?" the man asked.

"I'm going with you, Daddy," the little boy said. "See? I am walking just like you are!"

The boy was practicing the age-old ritual of trying to walk in his father's footsteps. His little legs were stretched to the point that the boy was leaping at times in order to put each of his feet in the snowy footsteps of his dad.

"Where am I going?" the man thought. With tears in his eyes, he gathered the little boy in his arms and turned around. That night, he whispered to his wife, "I'm going forward," after Moody had given the invitation, and that man's life changed forever. So did his son's.

Do you remember the song Harry Chapin sang in 1974 that touched a nation's heart? It was called, "Cat's in the Cradle."

My child arrived just the other day, He came to the world in the usual way. But there were planes to catch, and bills to pay. He learned to walk while I was away. And he was talking 'fore I knew it, and as he grew, He'd say, "I'm gonna be like you, dad. You know I'm gonna be like you."

And the cat's in the cradle and the silver spoon, Little boy blue and the man in the moon. "When you coming home, dad?" "I don't know when, But we'll get together then. You know we'll have a good time then."

My son turned ten just the other day. He said, "Thanks for the ball, dad, come on let's play. Can you teach me to throw?" I said, "Not today, I got a lot to do." He said, "That's OK." And he walked away, but his smile never dimmed, Said, "I'm gonna be like him, yeah. You know I'm gonna be like him."

Well, he came from college just the other day, So much like a man I just had to say, "Son, I'm proud of you. Can you sit for a while?" He shook his head, and he said with a smile, "What I'd really like, dad, is to borrow the car keys. See you later. Can I have them please?"

And the cat's in the cradle and the silver spoon, Little boy blue and the man in the moon. "When you coming home, son?" "I don't know when, But we'll get together then, dad. You know we'll have a good time then."

I've long since retired and my son's moved away. I called him up just the other day. I said, "I'd like to see you if you don't mind." He said, "I'd love to, dad, if I could find the time. You see, my new job's a hassle, and the kid's got the flu, But it's sure nice talking to you, dad. It's been sure nice talking to you." And as I hung up the phone, it occurred to me, He'd grown up just like me. My boy was just like me.

We only get one chance, dads, so let's make it count.

⋘✥⋙

Prayer: "Lord, help me live today with the understanding that my actions help shape my child's character."

Action: Talk with your oldest son about that song and ask his forgiveness if you have been too busy.

Little girls need their fathers

"Fathers, do not provoke your children to wrath,
but bring them up in the training and admonition of the Lord."
(Ephesians 6:4)

I took my younger daughter to the Father and Daughter Valentine Dance at the YMCA this past Saturday night. Susanna had two red dresses she could have worn, but chose to wear the one "that Daddy bought me," as she said to her mother. The dance started at 6:30, so that meant my little 7-year-old princess had to start getting ready at least by 3:00! She got her outfit together, complete with the pink gloves she had picked out to go with her red dress. She washed her hair and then patiently sat as her Mom put her curlers in. She fussed over her clothes and her shoes and finally her corsage. In the meantime, her Daddy was fussing and fuming over the Tar Heels, who looked like they had forgotten how to play defense and were going down in flames to archrival NC State. I got my black suit on (it matched my mood after the game), and my new red valentine tie, and escorted my daughter to her first dance.

We learned how to waltz, how to do the Foxtrot, and how to swing. We watched and laughed as others showed off their 'electric slides' and their 'chicken noodle soups.' (I had never heard of the latter, and to be honest, could not begin to tell you what they were doing when they were doing it). We laughed at each other, especially at me, a lot. Susanna giggled when I told her she was the prettiest girl there. She saw some of her friends and had short conversations with them. But mostly, she just wanted to be with her

Daddy. We sat together on the sidelines and sipped our punch and nibbled our M&M's. But we were never off the dance floor long. Susanna would not allow that. Her favorite thing we did all night was when I would take her hands in mine as she faced me, and she would slide under my legs and as she slid back out in front of me, I would lift her off the floor. "Do it again, Daddy!" she said over and over.

I was reminded of two things during this event Saturday night. First, I was reminded that, next to having a root canal done with no anesthesia while shopping all night at Wal-Mart, the next most painful experience for me is dancing. I am just not good at it. I still remember, painfully, when I had to dance in a Gallery Players production of "Can You Tell Me the Zip of That Faraway Land?" in 1983. There were guys in the cast who were just not able to get the dance steps at all. And then there was me. I was hopeless.

Second, I was reminded about how much little girls need their Daddy. They need us to be there for them, to be tender and affectionate with them, and to show them that they are worth more to us than a ball game or a night at home to rest or even the embarrassment of showing other guys how badly we dance. Little girls need their Daddy.

One day a young man is going to come calling, asking for my little girl's hand in marriage. Until then, I will keep her heart and protect her and love her. And who knows? I may even take her to the dance again next year. Her toes should be healed by then.

❧

Prayer: "Lord, help me love my little girl and give her what she needs from her Daddy."

Action: Plan a date with your daughter.

Thank God for friends like these

"Two are better than one ...
for if they fall, one will lift up his companion."
(Ecclesiastes 4:9,10)

Some of you may remember Steven Curtis Chapman's song, "The Walk."

The second verse says, "I got a friend named Larry; he sends me letters from a foreign land. He went there with his kids and his pretty wife, Mary, to answer a holy call ... they're just doing the walk."

I have a good friend named Larry, too. In fact, it's the same guy. Larry and Mary Warren were members of Antioch Church in the early 1990s, and we were privileged to ordain Larry and take part in sending him and his family to Africa.

He serves now as president of "African Leadership," and because of Larry's vision and God's grace, more than 30,000 African pastors have received two years of training in the Bible and church leadership.

The Warrens are doing "the walk" and thousands in 29 countries of Africa are reaping the benefits. But let me tell you about a different walk that the Warrens took a few years ago.

Mt. Kilimanjaro is the tallest free-standing mountain in the world, at 19,500 feet. The Warrens spent seven days climbing that mountain, but Larry and Mary almost didn't make it.

The last day of the climb was to begin at 10 p.m. and end the next afternoon at the summit. Larry asked why they would be climbing in the dark, not able to see where they were going. The guide answered, "Because if you could see where you were going, you would not climb!"

With only five hours to go to the summit, the guide had to make a decision. Some in the group were slowing the others down.

"I will separate the group into two, so that you can all keep up your pace and get to the top." Larry said the guide separated the 12 climbers into a group of ten, and a group of two: Larry and Mary. Seems they were slowing down the pack just a bit.

Two guides remained with Larry and Mary, and the others raced ahead toward the summit. Larry said that the last five hours were grueling, and he was praying that Mary would quit, so he could quit with her.

Finally, with three hours left, Mary was done.

"I can't go any further," she said to the guides.

"Can you go for 30 more minutes?" the guide asked.

Mary agreed she could, thinking that the summit was a half-hour away.

"He used that same line about five more times!" Larry said. But it worked to keep them motivated and moving. With only an hour to go to the top, Mary was completely worn out. That's when the guides did for the Warrens what we all need when it seems we cannot go on.

Larry said, "One went in front of us and Mary held onto his backpack. The second went behind her, pushing her on the back, and I came behind the second guide and held on as these men literally pushed and pulled us up the mountain.

"Yes, we kept walking. We did our part. We did the best we could, but it was the strength and determination of these experienced guides that helped us make it to the top."

was I thinking? I had been in the park every bit of an hour. I was there with my church group to have fun and to fellowship, and, as our youth director had reminded us, "to be a good witness." As I reflected on this while we walked toward the office, I just had this sinking feeling that my "witnessing technique" left a lot to be desired.

The other fatal flaw, which I realized as soon as the discussion started in the office, was that I was wearing a bright orange t-shirt. Apparently as soon as the gum left my hand and winged its way toward its intended target, trained professionals saw the falling object, followed the line of the trajectory back up to the cable car where I, Wonder Boy, sat with my right arm still dangling. They had me dead to rights.

If I had been thinking clearly, I might have taken these employees to the exact spot where they saw me from the ground, and proven that, given the angle of the sun as it was rising in the eastern sky, there was no way the accusers, who were facing east at the time could have seen me well enough to have identified me.

Then again, they probably had seen that same episode of "Andy Griffith." My ploy might not have worked.

Instead, I hung my head and confessed, feeling really sorry that I had gotten caught, and just a little sorry that I had done something wrong. The next thing I remember is the park employees escorting me to the entrance of the theme park, asking me to "make sure and have a nice day ... somewhere else." I deserved it.

The Bible says, "Foolishness is bound up in the heart of a child, but the rod of discipline will drive it far from him." I felt the sting of the Lord's rod that day, and found out once again that growing up is hard to do. But no matter the cost, it's worth it.

⋅⋅⋛⋙⋅⋅

Prayer: "Lord, help me to stand alone when those around me want to do what is evil."

Action: Talk with your children about the dangers of peer pressure. Read the story of Daniel and his friends who refused to eat from the King's table (Daniel 1)

Whatever fills you, controls you

*Make no friendship with an angry man,
and with a furious man do not go.
(Proverbs 22:24)*

Have you ever seen anybody who was filled with rage? The anger that fills them also controls them.

I remember the time as a teenager when I went on a double date with my cousin. Halfway through the date, I found out the girl I was with had an insanely jealous boyfriend.

He was also big, she said. "And," she added, "He has a nasty temper."

I figured that to be a deadly combination, so I filed that information away, reminding myself to avoid this boyfriend of hers at all costs. We were driving home later that night when all of a sudden my cousin said, "Uh-oh."

"What's the problem?" I asked, thinking maybe we were running out of gas.

"Don't look now," he said, "but Marty is right on our tail." I looked anyway and saw a car about 2 inches from our bumper, and we were doing 60 on the interstate.

"Who's that?" I asked. "Uh ... that's my boyfriend," the girl I was with answered.

"Uh-oh," I replied.

Now, up until this point I had only done one thing I regretted, and that was to go out with this girl in the first place. But now I became a willing participant in a series of stupid mistakes.

May I say to any teens who happen to be reading this: "Don't try this at home ... or on the interstate." My cousin floored the car (a 1972 Camaro Z-28) and we took off like a rocket. We were going over 90 mph with Marty right on our tail, and it is only by the grace of God, gentle readers, that I am here to tell the story.

We finally reached our exit, careened onto the ramp, and headed for my cousin's house. Marty was only seconds behind us. My cousin realized we weren't going to outrun him, so he said something like, "Good luck, Mark!"

I was shaking with adrenaline and fear, and could hear the words "big ... nasty temper ... insanely jealous" reverberating in my skull. My legs felt like Jell-O and my mouth was dry as dust.

About that time my cousin slammed on the brakes in his car-port, and I managed to fall out of the car to face my attacker, who was jumping out of his car as it slid to a stop in the driveway.

Now you have to realize that at this time in my life, I had not yet had my growth spurt. In fact, I still haven't had it, but I was a skinny 16-year-old then, only about 5' 6" and maybe 110 pounds soaking wet.

As I recall it, Marty seemed to tower over me by at least a foot. But what I remember most of all was the purple rage that consumed him. He was so filled with wrath that he had no control of his body.

He couldn't swing his fists because the anger controlled them. He couldn't speak, but sputtered and fumed, because the anger had his tongue.

As he stumbled toward me I bent over, and he pounded me on my back. The blows were nothing, dissipated by the rage that controlled him.

I saw something that day I will never forget. Whatever fills you controls you, whether it is wine, anger, lust, or greed. I am so thankful the Lord spared my life that day, but most of all I rejoice in the way he can take our anger and turn it into passion for him.

Prayer: "Lord, help me not to use anger to control my children or to get my way."

Action: If you have been angry with your children and not confessed, go to them and make it right. You may want to read the book of Jonah together and see how God dealt with Jonah's anger.

Meeting needs shows Christ's love

*"Inasmuch as you did it to one of the least of these my brethren,
you did it to me."*
(Matthew 25:40)

K atrina hit the Gulf Coast with a vengeance in August of 2005,
but the cleanup and the rebuilding continues. That's why I was
delighted to be able to go down with 11 others in the winter of
2007 to put in a few days of labor. We left at 4:30 a.m. on Monday,
and arrived in Kiln, Mississippi at 5:30 p.m., CST. The twelve in
our team included seven who were 21 years old or younger, and
five married men. The three young ladies in our group slept in the
Toddler's Room ("not potty trained") of the church, and the men
were in another Toddler's Room ("potty trained"). We definitely
got some mileage out of that. The church we stayed in, Bayou Talla
Fellowship, has opened her doors to Samaritan's Purse and basically said, "All that we have is yours." For 1 1/2 years, the church
has been the hub of operations for a huge Katrina relief effort. The
front and side yard look like a mobile home park, and nearly every
room of the church building is filled with volunteers who have
come to lend their backs to the effort. I found myself thinking, "If
disaster struck our city, would our church be as gracious?" I believe
we would, as would many other churches in the area, but I was
challenged by this self-sacrificing group in Kiln.

Every day started with breakfast at 6 a.m., prepared by a team
of volunteers who got to the church by 4:30 to cook eggs and

bacon, pancakes and toast, grits and coffee. Another team of volunteers would arrive at 4:00 p.m. to prepare a big supper for us. You know what is a crying shame? It is a sin, I think, to go on a mission trip and gain weight!

After breakfast and announcements, there would be a brief devotional, led by one of the SP staffers or a volunteer. The recurring message to us was, "You are not here to build houses, but to share the love of Jesus." Then all the teams would collect their tools and head out. I was working with six others from Antioch on a project 45 minutes away. The homeowner started building his own house last August, and it was ready for insulation and Sheetrock. I learned a lot about how to put in insulation, how to measure and cut the "rock," and how to apologize when I did both the wrong way. Repeatedly. By day three, I was at the point where I didn't have to be re-trained after each break.

One of the side benefits of going to a place like deep south Mississippi is the plethora of wild life. We had heard about the brown recluse and the black widow spider, the copperhead and the water moccasin, the mosquitoes (that obviously had not been told that it is winter). But what I had my sights set on was the good old American alligator. During lunch the first day, I asked the homeowner where the closest ones were. "'Bout 800 yards thataway, in the pond." I struck off down the road with a song in my heart and a vision of running from a 14-foot gator chasing me up the bank! Didn't see a one.

We got back Saturday, grateful for the opportunity we had that week to help meet a need, and to meet part of our family of faith.

✺

Prayer: "Thank You, Lord, that there are opportunities all around to help those who have needs. Help me to be faithful."

Action: Study Matthew 25:31-46 and see how you can help the hungry, the stranger, the sick, or the prisoner in your own community.

Practicing generosity can enlarge the soul

"The earth is the Lord's and all its fullness,
the world and those who dwell therein."
(Psalm 24:1)

A few years ago when we were enjoying a bit of "February summer," I took off with my three youngest into the woods around our house. We hiked for nearly two hours, got totally lost and had to find a creek and follow it until we found a road we recognized. We saw lots of flora and fauna, spotted a few deer stands, took a rest once as we sat on a deadfall tree and then laughed at each other as we tried to balance on it like we were trying out for the Beijing Olympics. It was a wonderful break from the normal routines of work and chores, and I thoroughly enjoyed wandering through the woods with my kids.

When we were following the creek to find a landmark we would recognize, we came up behind a house. I say "behind" the house: it was at least 300 yards from us. Between us and the house was what looked like a little private landfill, with some old appliances and tires that had been tossed onto a pile. There was lots of undergrowth, some trees, and then the yard of this house started. So, you get the picture? We were not really anywhere near the house, just passing along behind it in the woods. As we laughed and walked along beside the gently flowing creek, my eye caught movement. I looked up to see a man who appeared to be in his 60s, hustling toward us as though he were on a mission. He kept his eye on us as he made his way from the house and across the back yard. I could tell he wanted to say something to us, so I stopped walking and motioned for my three children to stop. "Hello! How are you?" I called out to the stranger with a smile on my face.

"This is posted land," he said, grimly. "You need to move on off of it."

"That's what we're doing," I said, again with a smile. But my heart sank as I stood there with my 6-year old daughter, and two sons ages 12 and 10. I mean, we didn't exactly look like a rookie league for the Hell's Angels, searching for a house to burn down as an initiation rite. We were a middle-aged man with three kids, on a hike in the woods, for crying out loud! The rebel in me rose up for just a moment, and I had to bite my tongue as I resisted saying something I shouldn't to this poor man. I just said, "Let's go, guys," and we walked on.

I thought about what the Bible says: "The earth is the Lord's and all its fullness, the world and those who dwell therein." The truth is, with all due respect to Woody Guthrie, this land is not your land or my land. It is His land. The Lord owns it all.

One of the most exciting transformations happens when we 'transfer ownership' of all of our stuff, including our land and our house and our health and our money, to the Lord. When we give back to Him what is rightfully His, not only will He use it for His own glory, but the Lord will give us great delight in holding things loosely and loving Him and His people lavishly.

Miserliness shrivels a man's heart, but generosity enlarges a man's soul.

◈◈◈

Prayer: "O Lord, make me a giver, like You are a giver!"

Action: Transfer ownership of your property into the Lord's name and talk to your children about the meaning of being a good steward.

We are all part of the family

"...that they all may be one, as You, Father, are in Me,
and I in You
(John 17:21)."

It was Sunday morning, Aug. 1, 1999. Cindy and I were at the hospital, in labor and delivery room number 5.

Cindy was in the final moments of delivering our seventh child, and at precisely the same time, Jesse (our fifth) was having a convulsion on the front row at Antioch Community Church.

I know that sounds like a line right out of Erma Bombeck, but it really happened. His fever spiked at 11:19 a.m. and he convulsed.

A visiting missionary was about to preach but when he saw what was happening, he immediately began praying. Others in the church flooded the front and began to pray for Jesse.

Our friend John was trying to hold Jesse's tongue down, but neither the tongue nor the teeth were cooperating and John's fingers suffered the results.

Someone called 911 and within five minutes, firemen were running through the front door of the building.

A minute later, EMTs were racing in.

Their first question was, "Who's the Mom?"

Martha replied, "She's at the hospital, having a baby." Martha had just called and spoken with me about Jesse. The EMT said, "Well, I need to call and talk with her." Martha replied, "She's pushing. I don't think that's a good idea." "Well, then, who's the next of kin?" the EMT persisted. John piped up, "I am. We're all family, here!" John, my brother in Christ, gave them permission to treat Jesse, and the EMTs went to work. All was settled, finally, and the worship service resumed. By the time the service was over, all had dried their tears for Jesse, and he was sitting up and taking nourishment. Then Micah (our oldest) announced to the church that Susanna Joy had been born, and everyone began to cry again. That day's events confirmed to me what I have known for a long time. We truly are family in the body of Christ. There is a bond that is deeper than the blood of natural kinship. It is the bond of the spirit, the bond of faith that makes us one, not just for this life but for the life that is to come.

Bill and Gloria Gaither's chorus sang, "I'm so glad I'm a part of the family of God, I've been washed in the fountain, cleansed by His blood. Joint heirs with Jesus as we travel this sod, for I'm part of the family, the family of God."

I would not trade anything for the family of God. That family extends beyond our local church, of course, and reaches around the world.

I have brothers in the Kibera slum in Nairobi, for example. I have slogged through the mud during rainy season in Kenya to preach at their churches. The first church I preached in there had a corrugated tin roof that leaked like a sieve. The walls were card-board, the floor was dirt. But the people there, my family members, were filled with a joy in the Lord that is rare in America. They sang loudly and danced with exuberance, worshiping Jesus with all their might.

I have been back three times and taken two sons and one daughter to meet some of their brothers and sisters in Africa. And why not? We are family.

❧✿❧

Prayer: "Lord, thank you for placing me and my family in our local church, and for the family of God around the world to which we are connected."

Action: Pick a family or single person in your church and pray for them with your children. Invite them over for a meal to let them know you love them.

Fathers are given a clear purpose

"Most assuredly, I say to you, the Son can do nothing of Himself,
but what He sees the Father do..."
(John 5:19)

The first time I visited Kenya and went with our mission team to Masai Mara in the southern part of the country, I was enthralled. The Masai village we visited consisted of 10 huts, each built with sticks, mud and cattle dung. They are arranged in a tight circle, and the only entrance into the village is through a gate, which is closed and guarded at night. As we walked in and were welcomed by the Masai warriors (dressed in traditional red, many carrying clubs, one wearing a lion's mane as a headdress), we had to be careful not to step on cattle dung. The Masai gave us their traditional welcome dance, forming a circle and taking turns leaping as high as they could as the others chanted a greeting to the visitors. After the welcome, they gave us a tour and explained the life of the Masai.

Let me say to any women who are reading that you can thank God every day you were not born Masai. The first thing a Masai woman must do after she gets married is build the house where she and her husband will live. Then her day consists of tending the children, fetching the firewood, cooking the meals, cleaning the house, and making repairs on it when necessary. You're thinking the same thing I am, aren't you? What does the man do?

I asked a Masai warrior that question, and he looked at me like I was from another planet. Then he said, very seriously, "We protect the village." He had a point. This was lion country, and lions love Masai cattle. That's the other thing Masai men do; they take care of the hundreds of cattle that each village owns. There's one more thing the Masai men take very seriously: they train young Masai boys to become men.

As we drove through Masai territory I saw little boys, no older than 4 or 5, herding chickens around with a stick. I saw older boys, maybe 9 years old, taking care of a herd of goats. The young teenage boys were taking care of a small herd of cattle. Almost as soon as a little Masai boy is weaned, he is sent to work with Daddy. He learns the skills of his father, learns to hunt and kill predators, learns to protect the village, learns to be a man. A 10-year-old Masai boy can throw a club with great accuracy from 30 feet and hit a lion or hyena that has crept into the area. I was told that when a lion sees a Masai walking across the savannah, carrying his spear and his club, the lion turns and goes the other way.

So when I asked how many of the young men grow up and leave the Masai culture and move into the cities, the man I asked looked at me like I had just asked how cows feed their young, like what I said was *udderly* ridiculous. He replied with a scowl, "Almost none leave." "Why not?" I persisted. He said firmly, "Because they know they are Masai."

I believe it is universally true: those who understand their purpose and their calling will not abandon their posts. We fathers who follow Christ are given a clear purpose when it comes to our own children. Are we standing firm, manning our positions, doing the great work of fatherhood?

May God help us be faithful.

◈

Prayer: "Lord, help my children to know very early what their purpose is, and to remain faithful to You all the days of their lives."

Action: Talk around the supper table about what our life purpose is, and ask each child to share what he believes God is calling him to.

Dad Was a Fighter

*"But now Christ is risen from the dead,
and has become the firstfruits of those who have fallen asleep."
(1 Corinthians 15:20)*

My Dad was born Oct. 19, 1935. He was too young to fight in World War II, and too young to fight in the Korean War. He was too old — and too married — to fight in the Vietnam War.

He always regretted not being a veteran, but don't get the wrong idea that my Dad wasn't a fighter. He was. Oh, my goodness, he was.

Dad grew up in an auto mechanic's home that boasted one bathroom for eight children and two parents. His dad couldn't afford to send him to college, so Dad went to work right out of high school and fought his way up the corporate ladder.

He believed in excellence in everything he attempted, and this certainly applied to his job. Dad was respected and sought after by all who worked with him, including those who moved past him on the ladder because of their college degrees.

Dad was a fighter in the community, taking the lead in helping to build a community center that included a pool and tennis courts. He was named the Old Town Civic Club man of the year in 1972 and was proud of the recognition he was given for his efforts.

Dad was a fighter in the church, helping to build Old Town Baptist Church as one of 35 charter members, along with my mom.

He served there as a deacon, a Sunday School teacher, a member of the choir, and he led the way in raising money for the church to build a larger sanctuary.

Dad was a fighter on the golf course. After he retired, he played five days a week with his "gangsome." He was hard to play with sometimes because he demanded so much of himself and every misplayed shot was met with lots of analysis and grief.

I truly believe my dad harbored a dream of one day playing on the senior tour.

Dad was a fighter in his marriage. He was married to his best friend for 51 years, but they had also been in the same class in every one of their 12 years at Old Town School. He and my Mom loved each other more than any two people I have ever known.

Dad would do anything for his sweetheart. That's why the news of his kidney cancer that came last September was such a blow. I saw my dad weep for the first time in my life as he said to his three sons, "I am going to fight this. I need to stay alive for your mother."

Dad's hardest fight came at the very end, when cancer attacked his body with a vengeance and his 6-foot-3 frame dropped below 120 lbs. He fought cancer, and death itself, more than anybody I have ever known, not because he was afraid to die, but because of his tremendous love for life.

He loved his wife and his garden and his golf game and his friends and family so much that he did not want to leave any of it behind.

At the age of 70, on a Sunday afternoon, just a few hours after Phil Mickelson won his second Masters Golf Tournament, my Dad met his Master. He made his triumphal entry into heaven. I know he is there because the Bible says that we who are followers of Jesus Christ are confident and willing "to be absent from the body and to be present with the Lord."

My Dad's fight is over. But his life has only just begun.

❦

Prayer: "Lord, teach me to number my days and to gain a heart of wisdom."

Action: Read through Psalm 90 with your children and discuss life and the finite number of our days on the earth.

Store up treasures in heaven

"Do not lay up for yourselves treasures on earth…"
(Matthew 6:19)

A round Christmas time one year, my six-year-old brought an American Girl catalogue to her mother. "Mom," Susanna said as she pointed to it, "if I could have everything on this page, I would be happy."

Cindy sat down with our youngest and explained to her how our hearts are almost never satisfied. "The more you have, Susanna, the more you will want." Susanna seemed to understand and went outside to play.

John Wesley once rode on horseback for hours over a huge estate with the plantation owner. They did not see all of it, so vast was the property. Over dinner that night, the land baron proudly asked, "Well, Mr. Wesley, what do you think?" The evangelist replied, "I think you're going to have a hard time leaving all this."

The problem with the stuff that most of us spend our lives trying to attain is that every bit of it ends up at the landfill. It all rots or fades or rusts or falls apart. Not only that, but before it falls apart it consumes all of our waking hours taking care of it, maintaining it, refinishing it, tuning it up, washing it, babying it, tinkering with it. Then it falls apart anyway!

W. H. Vanderbilt said, "The care of 200 million dollars is enough to kill anyone. There is no pleasure in it." Many of you will read that and think to yourself, "Old Vandy might have struggled with having riches, but not me. Just let me try it for a year, or even a month!" The Bible says, however, "Those who desire to be rich fall into temptation and a snare, and into many foolish and harmful lusts which drown men in destruction."

That doesn't sound like "the good life" to me.

In his book, The Treasure Principle, Randy Alcorn writes that people often say, "I want to have a heart for missions." Alcorn responds, "Jesus tells you exactly how to get it. Put your money in missions and in your church and in helping the poor, and your heart will follow."

Jesus said "where your treasure is, there your heart will be also." Those who say they want to have a heart for missions must put their money where their mouth is ... and their heart will come along! Not only that, but they will be storing up treasures in heaven, where "no thief approaches nor moth destroys."

Most Americans continue to pursue the elusive "dream," however, even at the expense of the true treasures that languish around their feet. According to the PBS special, "Affluenza," the average American shops 6 hours a week while spending 40 minutes playing with his children.

My investments on this side of eternity are meager, even laughable by many standards. But I am excited to see how my "Eternal Mutual Funds" will have appreciated by the time I reach heaven. The fund manager has promised me that if I lay up treasures in heaven, He will take good care of them for me. There is no risk involved but there is a tremendous payout that will be a blessing to me and to all those my giving was able to touch.

As for Susanna, I think she must have learned something from her Mom's encouragement that day. Just a few weeks ago a little girl said to Susanna that she wished she was rich so she would have lots of toys. Susanna told her Mom about it later and said she thought about saying to the girl, "The more we have, the more we want."

That's a treasure to me.

꧁❀꧂

Prayer: "Lord, thank you that life does not consist of those things we can hold in our hands!

Action: Read "The Treasure Principle" and discuss it with your children.

Fathers need to be better leaders

"You shall teach them diligently to your children..."
(Deuteronomy 6:7)

More than 400 people attended a "Uniting Church and Family" conference in Raleigh, NC a few years ago.

I met people from Florida, New Mexico, Texas and Ohio, eager to learn how the church can unite and encourage families.

One of the problems in the church today, I believe, is that fathers are not taking a leadership role in their homes, teaching their children the Bible. Part of the blame for that lies with the church, but part of it lies with Dad himself.

"The problem is," one speaker said, "too many men have PMS — Passive Male Syndrome."

I laughed as my mind immediately interposed the words and I thought of another growing problem in America today that affects both men and women — Massive Pale Syndrome, which is a result of staying indoors and eating lots of fatty foods.

Passive Male Syndrome, as the speaker described it, is the tendency that men have to sit idly by as their families struggle for lack of leadership. He said, "Men should not just be repositories of truth, but they should be dispensers of it as well,"

If you are a Christian father, you may be saying to yourself, "I would love to teach my family the Bible, I just don't know how." I have good news for you today. It is easy.

You start by simply reading the Bible aloud with them every day. Start with a book like the Gospel of John, and read a chapter aloud, each person in the family taking turns reading a few verses at a time. Or you can start with Genesis, or with the Bible's manual for child training, the book of Proverbs.

Just start somewhere and read a little at a time, every day, out loud, as a family. Bring the baby and the toddlers in, too. You will be amazed at what they can learn from the word of God.

"OK," you say, "I'm with you so far. We start by reading the Bible out loud as a family. Then what do we do?"

Friend, if you begin to do just that much, you will have moved into the rarefied air of families who actively seek to place the Bible in the center of what is taught, modeled, and encouraged in your home.

Begin by reading the chapter in Scripture. Then ask the family if anyone has a comment or a question about what was just read. You have to be careful here, because wrong thinking about the truth of God's word can lead to all kinds of error in doctrine and morality.

If your child asks you a question that you can't answer, the best response is, "I don't know, but I will find out."

Call an older brother in the church that has walked with the Lord longer than you, and ask him. Call an elder or your pastor. Search the Bible for answers, because the best commentary on Scripture is other Scripture.

Perhaps most important, pray. God delights in hearing his children ask for wisdom. "If any of you lack wisdom, let him ask of God." (James 1:5).

If you do these things, I believe you will see great changes taking place in your family.

Who knows? Maybe the church will even put an end to Passive Male Syndrome. That's my prayer.

❧❀❧

Prayer: "O Lord, help me to walk with purpose today with regard to my responsibilities as a husband and a father."

Action: Begin today, if you have not already, to have daily devotions with your family. Start to read through a book of the Bible, one chapter at a time, or even a paragraph at a time!

No frontier is tamed without discipline

*Now no chastening seems to be joyful for the present,
but painful; nevertheless, afterward it yields the peaceable fruit
of righteousness to those who have been trained by it."
(Hebrews 12:11)*

When our son Judah was 3, he liked to pretend he was Davy Crockett or Daniel Boone. He would dress up in his buckskins, don his coonskin cap, take 'ol Betsy and his powder horn, and head off into the backyard to trap and shoot wild animals.

Since we lived in downtown Graham at the time and our backyard consisted of a little bit of grass, a small garden, a swing set and a few trees, Judah had to use his imagination.

The wildest animal we ever encountered in our yard was a family of possums who decided to take up residence under our back deck. So, Judah mainly shot at invisible mountain lions and imaginary bears. That was hard work, though, and after a while, a frontiersman out in the wild works up a powerful appetite, so Judah Crockett would come in for supper.

The problem was, the grub was not always what a pioneer like Judah was expecting.

"Broccoli? Davy Crockett doesn't eat broccoli!" Judah said when he spied the unholy vegetable on his plate.

"He does if he wants to hunt mountain lions," his mother replied. "Broccoli gives pioneers energy and strength, and besides, you have to eat it. If you don't, you will have it for breakfast in the morning. And I don't think Davy Crockett ever ate broccoli for breakfast. Yuck!"

Judah Crockett was caught on the horns of a dilemma. "Do I eat the broccoli now, so I can hunt lions and bears in the morning after a good breakfast of eggs or cereal?"

He pondered that option. "Or do I refuse to eat it and hope that Mom will forget about it in the morning?"

Judah refused the broccoli, and was told that he would see it again in the morning. He slept fitfully that night, dreaming that he was Davy Crockett and he was being attacked by a giant broccoli tree that kept trying to eat him up. But when he woke up, the sun was shining, the lions and bears were out there, waiting to be trapped or shot, and Judah hit the floor with a smile, excited about life on the frontier.

When he got to the chow hall, drawn by the smell of cooked pork, he saw the rest of the family sitting down to a scrumptious breakfast of eggs, bacon and toast, and then the dream he had all night became a nightmare. His plate was there, and all that was on it was last night's broccoli.

"Where's my breakfast?" Judah asked, knowing the answer but hoping maybe that this was all a cruel joke.

"Right there," his mother replied. I added, "Judah, you were told last night what the deal was. If you want to be able to go outside and play this morning, you are going to have to eat your broccoli."

Judah slumped in his seat, his chin on his chest, his hands hanging at his sides, defeated on the outside but stubborn as the wildcats he hunted on the inside.

"I won't do it," he thought. "I will not eat my broccoli. Yuck!"

The lions and the bears had the run of our backyard that day because Judah Crockett's will remained strong until late afternoon. He finally gave in, and he learned two valuable lessons that day, that we are his parents whom he has to obey, and that discipline does produce good fruit!

❦❧

Prayer: "Lord, help me to be consistent, firm and loving in the discipline of my children."

Action: Set a good example by praising the cook and the meal at the supper table tonight!

Mothers remain heart of the home

"Her children rise up and call her blessed..."
(Proverbs 31:28)

Are moms important?

Well, I guess it depends on who you ask. The California State Judiciary Committee must not think moms are such a big deal. They passed a bill through their committee a few years ago that would remove sex specific terms such as "mom" and "dad" from textbooks.

The bill is sponsored by Democratic Sheila Kuehl, best known for playing Zelda Gilroy in "The Many Loves of Dobie Gillis" in the 1960s.

Kuehl, who is a lesbian, is quoted on WorldNetDaily as saying the aim of the legislation is to "improve the climate in schools for gay, lesbian, bisexual and transgender kids."

We have come a long way from the days of "Father Knows Best" and "Leave it to Beaver." A cartoon in the Saturday Evening Post years ago showed a young boy of 5 or 6 talking on the phone, saying, "Mom is in the hospital, the twins and Rozie and Billie and Sally and the dog and me and Dad are all home alone."

That was a time when moms were held in high esteem by most in our nation. Mom was the heart of the home, Dad was the head. Moms were the tender-hearted nurturers, dads the fearless warriors.

They made quite a team, Mom and Dad. They were incomplete without each other; his strengths were her weaknesses, her strengths were his weaknesses. Dad was too harsh sometimes, Mom was too soft. Together they raised children in a safe place. Not a perfect place, mind you. But one that was secure.

There are millions of children in the country today who would give anything to be in a home like that. In his book, "Love Must Be Tough," James Dobson tells the story of a sixth-grade teacher in California who taught in an affluent area. She gave her students a writing assignment.

They were to complete the sentence that began, "I wish ... " She expected the boys and girls to wish for bicycles, dogs, laptops and trips to Hawaii. Instead, 20 of the 30 children made reference to their own disintegrating families. Here's what some of them wrote:

"I wish my parents wouldn't fight and my father would come back."

"I wish my mother didn't have a boyfriend."

"I wish I could get straight A's so my father would love me."

"I wish I had one mom and dad so the kids wouldn't make fun of me."

I am so thankful for the mom who lives in my house. I couldn't imagine life without her. She truly is the heart of her household, and as the Proverb says, "The heart of her husband safely trusts her." That's why she deserves anything I and the kids give her tomorrow. No gift is too good for the mom who lives and loves at our house.

I heard a story about a boy talking to a girl who lived next door.

"I wonder what my mother would like for Mother's Day," he said.

The girl answered, "Well, you could decide to keep your room clean and orderly. You could go to bed as soon as she calls you. You could brush your teeth without having to be told. You could quit fighting with your brothers and sisters, especially at the dinner table."

The boy looked at her and said, "Naah, I mean something practical."

❦

Prayer: "Thank you for my wife and the mother of our children, and bless her for the sacrifice she makes to help take care of the household."

Action: Don't wait for Mother's day to spend some time going around the around the dinner table, praising the lady of the house for all that she is and does. Do it tonight!

Raising adults, not children

"...but diligence is man's precious possession."
(Proverbs 12:27)

Several years ago, my older daughter walked into the bedroom to ask an honest question about meal preparation. "Mom," she began, "What should I use to serenade the chicken?"

I couldn't resist.

I suggested, "Hey, Good lookin', whatcha got cookin'?" I know, I know, I'm a wise guy. After we had corrected her and pointed out that the word is "marinade," I went out and sang a few tunes to the bird anyway. I think I softened it up a little, and I also had fun laughing with my daughter, one arm around her as I sang and she chuckled at her mistake. She went on and cooked a delicious meal for the family.

I remember the time when our oldest son was having some attitude problems when it came to doing work around the house. He was probably 4 years old at the time, and Cindy suggested that he sing while he worked. "It will make the work go by faster, and you might even enjoy it," she said. And do you know that to this day, Micah whistles or sings while he works? I have heard that the carpenters he works with in the summer have asked him to take singing lessons, but that's another story.

Then there was the time I looked out the window and saw Micah teach his brother, Caleb, how to mow the yard. A few years later, Caleb was teaching his brother Luke. Then Luke taught Jesse, and now Jesse and Judah do it together. One final example: I came home from work one day and my little girl ran to meet me at the door, beaming with pride as she announced, "Dad, I asked Mom a question today about a million times!" I smiled and said, "Susanna, please don't ask Mom the same question more than once." One of the other kids chimed in, "No, Dad, she asked Mom if she could help her with anything."

Each of these examples is meant to illustrate a desire of my heart to raise adults at our house, not children. Cindy and I want our sons and daughters to grow up with a heart for serving others.

It has been established clearly that young adults who excel in the workplace are the ones who were trained at home by loving parents who teach a healthy work ethic. Those who stand out in business are most likely those who learned at home how to tackle any task with immediate and cheerful obedience. Those who have an "excellent spirit," like Daniel of old, will rise to the top. But the most important reason we are training our children to serve is because we want them to follow the lead of the Lord Jesus who said, "For even the son of man did not come to be served, but to serve, and to give his life a ransom for many." (Mark 10:45).

David Gergen, who served as an advisor to four U.S. presidents, tells the story of his first year in the Navy, right out of Harvard Law School. He was given the job of walking the admiral's dog, complete with pooper-scooper. And it was President Harry Truman who said, "It is not important that you have the best job — but that you do the best with the job that you have."

Even if that job is just to sing to the chicken!

⋘⚜⋙

Prayer: "Lord, help me to be a servant to my family and to teach my children how to serve. Remind me daily that they will follow my lead!"

Action: You may want to set up a reward system for the chore list, in which each child receives payment of some kind for the daily and weekly chores he or she performs with excellence, timeliness and good attitudes.

Resist the tyranny of the urgent

"Martha, Martha, you are concerned about many things,
but only one is necessary."
(Luke 10:41)

One of my favorite memories from childhood is really a collection of memories around the same theme. They happened at the beach, usually Surfside Beach, which is just below Myrtle. My family went there every summer and stayed in a cottage on the second row or beyond. On a rare occasion we would stay on the oceanfront. But it didn't matter to us where we were, as long as we were at the beach.

We would try to get on the road at 4 a.m. or so, to beat the heat and the traffic. We had a station wagon, I remember, brown, plain, with no air conditioning. Not many had AC in their cars in 1962.

Mom still tells the story of the time when I was just a toddler and we were on our way to the beach. Dad almost always stopped at the same Texaco service station in Rockingham, N.C. to gas up the car and let me and my brothers go to the bathroom. But when he stopped this time, I thought we were at Surfside. I jumped out the car with my bucket and shovel and started digging in the sandy parking lot, happy as a clam.

The days at the beach started with a leisurely breakfast. We would stake out our place on the sand no later than 9 a.m. and be out there until 4 or so. I would catch sand fiddlers, play Frisbee or baseball with my brothers, swim, body surf, and look for shark's teeth. My Mom was the world's best at finding shark's teeth, and she taught me how to look for them myself.

We ate seafood at Murrell's Inlet almost every night. Back then you could get a combination platter that was enough for 2 or 3 people for $5.99. We would sit and eat, and after supper my parents and grandparents would drink coffee and tell stories. They would recount memories from past vacations, and we never got tired of hearing the same tales every year.

We would finally stretch and push away from the table and make the trek back to our beach house. Sometimes we would pick up right where we left off at the restaurant, telling stories, enjoying each other's company with the sound of the waves crashing in the dark.

Don't get me wrong. There were also "special times" at the beach when we would go into Myrtle and ride the rides, or we would play Jungle Golf together. But those are not the memories etched on my heart, even if at the time they seemed more exciting than just hanging out with my family. No, what I remember most and best are simple times of eating together, laughing, and hearing about the past.

You know, as I think about it, some of my favorite memories from childhood that were not vacations were the many nights we sat under a dogwood tree in my grandparents' front yard and talked until we couldn't see each other any more. My grandfather would smoke his pipe and he and "Nana" would tell stories about what life was like when they were growing up.

I wonder sometimes, as we are running between baseball practice and Bible study, as we are getting ready for this play or that recital ... are we "doing" so much that the really important memories are not being made?

❧❀❧

Prayer: "Lord, help me not to be consumed by the 'urgent' at the expense of the important. Lift up my eyes, Lord, to see the vineyard right around me that needs my attention."

Action: Have a family meeting tonight and tell stories about how you grew up and some life lessons you learned. Your children will beg for more!

Laziness is an irritant to hard-workers

*"As vinegar to the teeth and smoke to the eyes,
so is the lazy man to those who send him."
(Proverbs 10:26)*

I had the privilege to work in an R.J. Reynolds factory during the 1970s. They had a program where employees' children who were in college could work for the summer. My job was to help put together "hogsheads," huge barrels that held 1,000 lbs. of tobacco. I worked with Terry, a young man who started at RJR right out of high school. He was friendly enough to me, but I could tell he was checking out this "college boy" to see if I was going to be able to handle the work. When I first started, I was slow and clumsy with the barrels. I had to wrestle each one into submission to get the pins in the sides. It was hard for me to pick up the round bottoms that we would throw into each hogshead before we rolled them over to the production line. And when I tried to roll one of the hogsheads to Terry, who was waiting for them 30 or 40 feet away, my efforts for the first several weeks were pitiful. There was no telling where the barrels would end up when I let them go. We would angle them toward us and roll them like one would a garbage can, so they stayed upright and tilted, spiraling to their destination.

Terry was patient with it, and me, and it paid off.

By the end of the summer I could keep up with Terry as we put the hogsheads together. I could throw the lids (which weighed 15 lbs. and were 48 inches in diameter) across three rows of hogsheads so they fell neatly into their targets. I could roll a hogshead from one end of the factory floor to the other and even learned how to spin them right into the empty slots. Hard work and a good teacher had produced an employee who contributed to the effort, and I went back to college at the end of the summer satisfied that I had learned something, grown in character and made some new friends.

There was another college boy working at the factory one of those summers. I heard the guys talking about him in the break room one day.

"I tell you what, that is about the height of laziness," one of the older men said, between swigs of a Pepsi. "Did you see 'college boy' out there on the floor?"

They were talking about the other college kid. He had been given the job of painting the guard rails in the factory that separated the floor area from the walkway around the perimeter. He was observed that day lying on his side on the floor, slowly moving his paintbrush to cover the guardrails with a neon yellow spread. It took him until lunchtime to paint ten feet of rail. At times it was hard to tell he was alive, his movements were so slow.

"I tell you what, if my boy was that sorry," the man continued, his eyes flashing, "I wouldn't let him out in public. That college boy is pathetic." The older man continued to complain and was joined by others in the room, who shook their heads in disgust. Laziness may not be a deadly communicable disease, but it sure does irritate everyone who is exposed to it!

❧❀❧

Prayer: "Lord, I have a natural tendency to want to rest when I should be working. Help me, Lord, to do whatever my hand finds to do with all my might!"

Action: Tackle that project or chore that your wife has put on your honey-do list and you have been putting off.

The price of disobedience

*"Who is so great a God as our God?
You are the God who does wonders..."
(Psalm 77:13,14)*

I was probably 6 years old, and it was the day before my family was going to the beach for summer vacation. We went to Surfside Beach for a week every year, and my grandparents were almost always there, and sometimes cousins and friends as well. It was the highlight of my year and I looked forward to every minute that we could run on the sand, play in the surf, watch the ships come in at Murrell's Inlet, and eat fresh seafood in one of the many restaurants there.

I remember this particular trip because it was the most miserable. All of the pictures that I appeared in feature a little boy covered in pink lotion from head to foot. Looking miserable. Making everybody else around him miserable.

You see, the day before we were to leave for the beach, I went outside to play. There was a pasture behind our house, surrounded by barbed wire. I would often crawl under or over the fence and run in the pasture, which was fine with Mom. This particular day, however, she didn't want me in the pasture.

"Mark, stay out of there!" she called from the carport.

I made a face and scampered under the fence.

"Mark, you had better stay away from the poison oak!" Mom yelled, not having the energy to even deal with my first disobedient act.

Now, you need to understand that when I was a boy, I could walk into a yard that was adjoined by a garden that was adjacent to a pond that was beside a patch of woods that had poison oak in it…and the next day I would be swollen up like a puffer fish. That's how badly I was allergic to the nasty little plant.

"You mean *this* poison oak?" I responded with glee, having pulled up handfuls of it as soon as she mentioned the weed. She looked on, aghast, as I proceeded to rub the noxious leaves over my face, neck, arms, and legs, as though I were bathing in the most luxurious spa in Paris. I crowed with delight when I saw the look on my mother's face. I beamed with pride at my little act of defiance. I had showed *her* who's boss, I thought.

This happened in the early 60's, and back then the only "cure" for poison oak that we knew about was calamine lotion. And that was no cure at all. It eased the misery a smidgen, but the sticky pink mess that was my body was the butt of every joke my two brothers could come up with. I couldn't enjoy being outside on the beach because the sun inflamed the fiery red ridges. I had to sit and watch as my brothers fished the surf with Dad. Even fried shrimp and french fries didn't taste the same. As we sat down to eat at Lee's Inlet Kitchen, people stared at this kid who was swollen and pink, marveling at how much poison oak could be on one little body. My bumps had bumps and my blisters oozed and ran, and my mind kept replaying that scene: "You mean *this* poison oak?"

I am amazed that God would choose to love and redeem such a rebellious boy as I. But the miracle of God's plan is not about how bad we are but it is about how great and forgiving He is.

If God can make something out of my life, He can do the same for anyone.

❧❀❧

Prayer: "Lord, show me my heart and where I still want to go my own way, delighting in willful rebellion at the expense of my character and my witness. Change me, Lord!"

Action: Write down the attitudes or thoughts or actions that the Lord brings to mind and commit each one to Him through repentance and faith.

Regular date nights keep marriage fresh

(She is) "A fountain of gardens, a well of living waters..."
(Song of Solomon 4:15)

I have been married to my best friend now for nearly half of my life. Cindy stole my heart the minute I laid eyes on her in Chapel Hill in 1981. I asked her to marry me on our second date; I was that sure that she was the one. She was, ahem, not as sure as I. Cindy needed more time to think and pray about it and make sure this skinny kid (that was pounds ago) with a dark tan and a loud laugh was the right one for her. She was worth the wait.

We got married in the summer of 1982 and lived on love for the first few years. As an advertising sales representative for a newspaper, married to a stay-at-home wife, I wasn't exactly known for my financial prowess. I remember our first Christmas together. I gave a $10 bill to her and one to myself. We separated in the mall and shopped until we had each found the "perfect present" for the other (meaning, "under $10"). We didn't mind that our little Christmas tree we had cut on a friend's farm had only a few, inexpensive presents under it. That was perhaps the simplest and the sweetest Christmas of my life.

As the years rolled on and children came into the picture, and life got busier and crazier, Cindy and I have maintained one simple practice that has made all the difference in our marriage. We have kept the weekly date alive.

Every week, usually on a Friday night unless it is softball season, you will find us out together for a few hours. In the days when our oldest child was under 12, it was difficult sometimes to find, or to afford, a babysitter. But God supplied. One year there were two teenage girls who offered to come every Friday afternoon and watch our children and even do some housework, while Cindy and I went on a date. The Lord knew just what we needed in that season of our life, and He provided. Since our oldest turned 12 more than 9 years ago, we have had live-in babysitters. The children look forward to when Mom and Dad are going on a date, because they usually fix a simple meal for themselves and watch a wholesome movie together while we're gone.

Our dates have not always required money. I remember many times when we just went to the nearby university and walked on the campus and talked, or we played tennis somewhere, or we even prepared a special meal and had a "date" together at home!

One thing I have learned over the years is that what my wife needs more than anything on our dates is to know that I love her and that she is my number-one priority. If our dates end up being a problem-solving session with something that's going on with me at the church, then one or both of us come away feeling like we didn't really have a date at all. One thing my wife has learned is that most of the time the last thing I want to do on our dates is shop. My idea of a good time does not have Wal-Mart or T.J. Maxx anywhere in it.

Solomon called his bride "a fountain of gardens, a well of living waters." Amen! I am thankful for the beauty and the refreshing that comes from being married to my precious bride. There is nothing so satisfying on this side of heaven.

ↂ

Prayer: "Lord, You have given me a treasure in my wife. Help me never to take her for granted."

Action: Plan a date with your wife for sometime this week. It doesn't have to cost anything except the time you give to it, and that will be a treasure to her.

Being a good father is worth the effort

"For I have known him, in order that he may command his children...that they keep the way of the Lord..." (Genesis 18:19)

I can relate to the Father's Day card that reads, "Dad, everything I ever learned I learned from you, except one thing. The family car really will do 110." It's a tough job being a father. Sometimes fathers get beat up on from all sides. Even at church. One little boy said to the preacher after the service, "Boy, that was a good sermon. My dad slumped way down today."

The truth is, there are no perfect fathers. The example of fatherhood that Jesus holds up is the father of the prodigal son in Luke 15, but even his home had struggles. So, what's a father to do? I believe a good place to start is with God's instructions to fathers in Deuteronomy 6:4-9. Here's a summary of how we apply it in our family.

First, we talk about Him when we sit in our house. We have family devotions every weekday morning, with God's help. It begins with Scripture and ends with us taking turns praying. We also try to eat most evening meals together (except on Friday night, when Cindy and I have our weekly date). During the family meals, I might ask the kids to tell me what they learned that day. Sometimes we will discuss the news of the day from a biblical perspective. I want my children to be like the "sons of Issachar who had understanding of the times..."(1 Chronicles 12:32).

We also talk about Him as we walk along the way. As we drive with our children in the car, we might use that time to ask them questions about what they believe, where they are in their faith, what their struggles and questions are. They are, after all, our most important disciples! I have had some of the most honest conversations with my children while riding alone with one of them and they feel free to let me into their lives.

We talk about Him as we lie down. One of our favorite things to do as a family is to read together before bed. We gather in the family room, each of us in a favorite chair or stretched out on the floor, and enter a different world together through books. We have been to the magical land of Narnia, into the slough of despair with Christian, onto the battlefields of Europe with Sergeant Alvin York, deep in the snowdrifts with the Ingalls, and plunged in the icy depths with the men and women of the Titanic. Our children learn from these books that suffering is part of God's plan, that Christ bids a man to come and die, and that nothing compares to His unspeakable joy. It's been said that we will all be the same five years from now except for the books we read and the people we meet. Our desire is that our children see Christ at work in the lives of great men and women of God and know that they are called to run the same race with endurance.

We talk about Him when we rise up. My oldest rises early now because he wants to, not because he has to. He looks forward to that time he spends with God before family devotions. My goal as a father is to raise seven adults who will love the Lord from their hearts, of whom it can be said, "The love of Christ compels them."

May God give each of you fathers great joy and wisdom as you pursue the high calling of fatherhood. It will be worth all the effort.

❧❀❧

Prayer: "Lord, give me wisdom to know what my children need, humility to bend myself to that task, and laughter in the enjoyment of these you have entrusted to my care for a few years."

Action: Choose a good book and begin to read it aloud to your family in the evenings before bedtime.

Don't run your life on auto pilot

"Watch, stand fast in the faith, be brave, be strong."
(1 Corinthians 16:13)

Once, when my second son was an infant, I laid him down on a kitchen countertop, just for a second, while I turned and opened the refrigerator door to get something. Hey, don't look at me like that. I was training my son to obey. I laid him down and said, "Caleb, stay there." I turned around, just for a second, and heard this sickening thud behind me. I turned back in horror to find my son lying on the kitchen floor, starting to cry. Then another voice (any guesses whose it was?) said, "Mark! What happened?" What happened was I took my eye off of my responsibilities, just for a second, and it could have been disastrous.

I remember when I was 17 years old, driving my father's Oldsmobile in Charlotte. I had gone there with two friends to check out colleges. I was driving down Independence Blvd., feeling like I might as well be in New York City, because I had never driven in traffic like that before. It was rush hour, I was nervous, driving with friends, not respecting the seriousness of the moment, and then it happened. I turned left at a stoplight right into oncoming traffic. A truck proudly owned by the Queen City hit us broadside and smashed up the Olds, and made an emotional wreck out of me.

That wasn't the worst of it. I ran over to the truck to see if he was OK and the driver waved it off, said, "Yeah, I'm fine," got out of his truck, assessed the damage, and got back in. I went back to my car and waited for the police to arrive. He did. As soon as he got there, the truck driver got out of his car and was limping like he had a compound fracture in his right femur! I told the officer that the man was fine two minutes earlier, but the officer told me not to worry about it. I didn't. I should have.

Six weeks later there was a knock at the door and my father was served with a lawsuit because of the wreck. I thought I was going to pass out. Again, the whole thing happened because I had taken my eye off of my responsibilities, just for a second!

I can't tell you how many times in 25 years of marriage I have found my wife crying because I have taken my eye off of my responsibilities and she has ended up having to carry something or take care of something that I was supposed to do. Some say that a woman notices when there is a leak in the roof, but the man only notices when the roof caves in. That can apply to actual leaks, or it can apply to problems with the finances, child discipline issues, problems with the marriage or with the spiritual environment in the home. Maybe that's why Paul said to the believers in Corinth, "Watch, stand fast in the faith, be brave, be strong."

"Watch." This is not a passive word that would describe something like watching television. If that is all that God is requiring of us, then the country is ablaze with his glory. People everywhere are watching, but not in a biblical sense. In fact, watching television is probably the exact opposite of what this word means. This word is a command to rouse, to wake up, to refrain from sleep, to engage in what is going on around you.

Are you watching, or are you on autopilot?

Prayer: "O Lord, keep me alert and awake to my responsibilities as a husband and a father; help me to deal with the 'leaks' before the roof caves in!"

Action: Ask your wife if there are any areas in the family that need your attention, and then follow through 'in the day you hear of it.'

Her worth is far above rubies

*"Who can find a virtuous wife? For her worth is far above rubies.
The heart of her husband safely trusts her"
(Proverbs 31:10-11).*

One day in graduate school at UNC, I found a Bible in the parking lot. When the owner came to get it, he said, "Hey, have you met the girls that live downstairs?"

He took me down and introduced me to the four roommates, but I only saw one that day. Her name was Cindy and she was the most beautiful girl I had ever laid eyes on. She still is. I didn't waste any time asking her out, and on our second date I didn't waste any time asking her to marry me. She said "I don't know," and kept me waiting for 4 months. One year after we met we were married and seven children and 25 years later, we are still in love. In fact, more so than we even knew possible back in those days.

That story plays such a pivotal role in my spiritual journey. You see, I had been engaged once before. It was a few years earlier. I woke up one morning as a first-semester senior at UNC and said to myself, "I am going to graduate in May. I have got to find a wife!"

That's about how deep the thought process went.

I was dating a UNC senior at the time, so I proposed and she accepted. I bought a wedding ring, she bought a wedding dress, and we began to make plans. But something in me was just not settled.

I didn't understand it, so I ignored it. Then I went home for Christmas.

I remember sitting in Sunday School class, and the teacher's subject was what he called "The Three M's." He said, "Before you choose a mate, you need to make sure that you know what your mission is. And before you choose a mission, you need to know who your master is. If you put the cart before the horse, you are going to have a big mess. You cannot know your mission unless you have surrendered to the master, the Lord Jesus Christ. And you are in no position to choose a mate unless you know what the Lord has called you to do."

That was a "two-by-four to the head" moment for me. It was like God was saying, "I have been trying to get your attention for a long time, Mark, and you just wouldn't listen."

You see, I had given my life to Jesus Christ as a teenager, and at the age of 15 I knew that He was calling me to preach the gospel. But when I got to college, I began to pursue my own agenda, and I ran as far away as I could from the calling and the relationship I knew was there. I spent lots of nights in Chapel Hill bars, and lots of nights running after the thrill of instant gratification. When I decided to find a wife as a senior in college, it was on my terms. I was my own master, and my mission at that point was just to have fun. Then the two-by-four shook me back to reality, and I had to do one of the most embarrassing things I had ever done, and break off an engagement.

I wish I had heard about "The Three M's" as a teenager, but I am so grateful that God woke me up before it was too late. Besides the Lord, I have no greater treasure than my bride of more than 25 years.

❧

Prayer: "Thank you, Lord, for giving me the wife You chose for me before the foundations of the world!"

Action: Write your wife a note or compose a poem or a song that expresses your love for her. Be ready to catch her when she starts to pass out! ☺

The first step is the hardest

*"...as soon as the soles of (your) feet...shall rest in the waters
of the Jordan, the waters of the Jordan shall be cut off...
and they shall stand as a heap"
(Joshua 3:13).*

There is a Chinese proverb that says, "A thousand mile journey must begin with the first step."

I remember when I sold World Book encyclopedias door to door to supplement my income as a pastor. The hardest thing to do every morning was get in the car and drive to a neighborhood and knock on strangers' doors. Everything in me militated against taking that first step out of the car. Sometimes I would sit in the car in front of a house for 5 or 10 minutes, until I was convinced that if I didn't go ahead and get out, the neighbors were going to be calling the police about this "guy sitting in the car like he's casing the neighborhood."

I would finally summon my courage, reminding myself of a wife, two children, and one on the way who were depending on me to put milk and bread on the table. Taking that first step out of the car and onto the sidewalk was all I needed. After that, it was easy. I didn't mind talking to the person who opened the door. I believed in my product and could sell it. Once I took that first step, I was OK.

The same thing happens to me when I get ready to write a column each week. I can easily spend 30 minutes just staring at my computer, trying to figure out what I should write about.

Sometimes that staring is made more productive through prayer, but I admit that sometimes it is closer to catatonia than conversation. But when I finally get started, once I take the first step, I am on my way and the words sometimes even seem to write themselves.

Taking the first step to inviting someone over from the church for dinner might be the key to building fellowship. Deciding you are going to really clean out the garage is not enough. You have to take the first step...into the garage! Making up your mind that you will witness to someone tomorrow is a great idea. But great ideas lay dormant unless and until the first step is taken. Having a desire to play the piano is epidemic. The numbers dwindle, however, when you count those who take the first step, or, lesson. Wanting to see your family settled into a good church is a wonderful 'want.' It will only happen when you turn that want into action and take the first step.

Sometimes taking the first step even results in God's miraculous intervention. Take the children of Israel and their entrance into the Promised Land, for example. God commanded the priests who carried the Ark of the Covenant to take the first step into the Jordan River. This was during flood stage so the water would have been deep and swift. The promise that would attend to their obedience was clearly spelled out by God's promise: "step in, and *then* the waters will obey Me." (my paraphrase)

That first step was the hardest because it required faith. But God enables us to act in faith and then God rewards faith with His power! The waters stood that day on either side like a wall of testimony to God's faithfulness.

What God has promised will come to pass, but sometimes He lays down conditions for His blessings. In this case, it was that His followers take the first step. It is not only the hardest step, but the most important one as well.

❧⚜❧

Prayer: "Lord, show me the first step and give me the courage to take it."

Action: Whatever the Lord shows you that needs to be acted on, take the first step!

Can Teens Love the Lord?

*"But Daniel purposed in his heart
that he would not defile himself..."*
(Daniel 1:8)

To celebrate her 18th birthday, my daughter Hannah wanted to invite a bunch of her friends and their brothers over to play volleyball. Thirty young people, ranging in age from 16 to 22, showed up at our house one Saturday afternoon and played speed volleyball for 4 hours. We learned about this variation on the game from Micah, our oldest, when he was in college. The idea is that you can have 5 or 6 teams playing (with only two on the court at the same time, of course). The team that misses the shot has to rush off the court while the next team in line rushes on before the serving team can hit it over. It is a lot of fun and very competitive if the teams are evenly matched.

Besides playing volleyball, these young folks roasted marshmallows over a bonfire and made s'mores. They talked about things that were going on in their lives, like their schoolwork or their jobs or their churches or their families. No one bragged about how much beer he had consumed the night before. No one talked about how many potential boyfriends she was stringing along. No one was complaining about his parents and the 'tyranny' of living within set boundaries. Not one word of profanity was used, even in the most frustrating of moments on the court.

Let me assure you that these were very normal, red-blooded teens and young 20-somethings. These were not angelic beings beamed in from heaven for an afternoon of recreation. But may I suggest to you that these young people were anything *but* normal? They weren't talking about the things teens normally talk about because that is not their lifestyle. I know every one of these kids and have for years. They love their parents and have good relationships with them. They love their siblings and, most of the time, are trying to be good examples for them. They love having fun and can spend an afternoon or evening completely sober and unimpeded by foreign substances and not feel like they "missed out" on anything.

The difference between these thirty young people and a random sampling of dozens more is very simple. They have given their hearts to Jesus Christ. They live for Him, not themselves. Like young Daniel, serving God in a foreign culture, they have purposed in their hearts not to defile themselves and be "squeezed" into the world's mold.

Jeff Baldwin, in his excellent book on worldviews entitled *The Deadliest Monster*, said "The difference between non-Christians and Christians is *not* that one acts selfishly all the time and one does not, but rather that one will often treat selfishness as a virtue while the other views selfishness only as a vice." The world teaches our young people to build their self-worth and their ethics on selfishness. If you don't believe that, just look at the billboards, listen to the radio spots and watch the commercials that reflect our nation's value system. The Bible teaches us to build our lives on selflessness. I was thrilled to hear Zach Johnson, the 31 year old winner of The Masters, give a testimony to Jesus Christ. There was no chest-thumping, no self-aggrandizement, no braggadocio. Just a simple and humble gratefulness to God and to all those who helped him make it to the Butler Cabin.

As the young people finished the volleyball games, hugged each other and headed home that Saturday, I couldn't help but marvel at their wholesome love for one another and for the Lord. That's sweeter than the best s'more!

❧✿❧

Prayer: "Thank you, Lord, for young adults in my family who love You and Your Word."

Action: Praise the teens in your house for walking with the Lord and help them plan a time for friends to come over (with their parents, if they can come) and play volleyball or another game that the teens will enjoy.

Children are a blessing

"Behold, children are a heritage from the Lord..."
(Psalm 127: 3)

Almost every time my whole family goes anywhere in public, it happens. There are stares. There are elbow jabs and subtle head nods in our direction. Sometimes people look like poorly trained mimes, pointing at each of us and counting silently, moving their lips, "one... two... three..."

There are sometimes even comments. "Are those all yours?" "Do you know what causes that?" And my favorite, "Do you have a parade permit?"

As I have said in previous entries, my wife and I have seven children. And to answer your questions, "Yes, they are all ours." "Yes, we know." "No, we don't need a parade permit, but that's funny."

Most of the time, people are curious or amazed. Every now and then, someone is genuinely appreciative of what they call our "courage." We were even shocked once many years ago when our waiter at a local restaurant told us, "Someone has picked up your tab. Your meal is paid for." We kept going to that restaurant every week for a year, hoping it would happen again, but ... not really.

There have also been the occasions, and they have been few and far between, when someone takes it upon himself to question our good sense, our ethics, or even our morality. I remember a woman asking us why we would have so many children at a time when the world is "running out of resources." I have been challenged by students who say, with all the sincerity in the world, that every family in America should be limited to two children.

A pastor from Texas said he was talking to a man he had just met, and the man introduced his three children as "Any, Minnie, and Miney." The pastor looked at him funny, so the man continued, "We ain't having no Moe."

All of those comments point to an almost universal belief in America: children are not a blessing, they are a burden. Children are seen in our culture by many as an optional extra. I have met people who told me that they were not having kids, they were having dogs instead. Why, I asked? Because kids are more trouble!

I hear people say things like, "I will be glad when summer is over so these kids can go back to school!" Or, "I cannot wait to have these kids grown and gone so I can have a life again!" Or even, "It's because of you kids that we don't have a nicer house!"

We have graduated two from high school and one from college, and our youngest is seven, so we have a long way to go. But my wife and I would not trade with anybody else in the world. We believe what the Bible says, that "children are a heritage from the Lord, the fruit of the womb is a reward." We believe that our lives have been richly blessed by our children, and that it will get even better as these young people we have trained in the fear and admonition of the Lord get married and begin to raise their own children. We believe that God will greatly use these young warriors to impact their culture with the gospel of Jesus Christ, and it doesn't get any better than that.

Who knows? Perhaps one day, when all of us, parents, children and grandchildren go out in public together, we will need a parade permit. I hope so.

❧

Prayer: "O Lord, my children are a blessing from You, not a burden, and I give You thanks for each one!"

Action: If you are not already in the habit, begin today praying for each of your children, by name, every day.

Lessons learned the hard way

"And whatever you do, do it heartily,
as to the Lord and not to men ... for you serve the Lord Christ."
(Colossians 3:23-24)

"I didn't mean to throw the cat, I really didn't. It was a reflex, that's all. I promise!"

I was 16 years old, working at the local veterinarian hospital. My responsibilities after school each day included cleaning up the cages, giving shampoos, holding an animal still while the doctor gave it a shot, and brushing out a cat or dog that was getting ready to go home.

It was that last detail that got me into trouble. I was holding a cat, getting ready to brush its fur because the owner was coming in a few minutes to pick it up. I wasn't hurting the cat, I wasn't squeezing the cat too hard, I was just holding the cat. I started to brush it out, as I had done with numerous dogs and cats before, when it bit me. That feline sunk its teeth into the thumb of my right hand, the one that was holding the brush. My left hand, out of reflex (and some sympathy for its partner, I am certain) went into immediate battle mode. It hurled the aforementioned cat across the room. Just as the doctor was walking in.

It may be true that cats have nine lives. But this cat didn't need them because the life it had was in good shape. It landed on its feet and ran under a table.

It is definitely not true that veterinarian's assistants have nine lives. My short-lived career in the field of veterinary medicine came to an abrupt end that day.

Now the cat lovers are no longer with us, I know. They stopped reading after my first sentence and went immediately to the computer to send me a nasty e-mail. But the rest of you may even be shocked at the swift, punitive action taken by the doctor. "I would have done the same thing if the cat had bitten me for no good reason," some of you are thinking, rallying to my defense.

Let me assure you this was simply the proverbial "straw," and I had already given the good doc plenty of reasons to let me go. My halfhearted work ethic and my less-than-cheerful disposition had already gotten me into trouble. This final cat-hurling episode proved to be my undoing.

I will never forget what the doctor said that day. "Mark, this is just a temporary stopping off place for you as you go through high school. But this is my career. Everything you do reflects on me and my practice. I am going to have to let you go."

I realized that not only had my poor work habits brought shame to the veterinarian, they had reflected badly on the Lord. The vet and his staff all knew that I was getting ready to preach for "Youth Sunday" at my church. They all knew I went to church every Sunday and yet my actions and my attitude at work preached a terrible sermon.

Getting fired that day was one of the best things that has ever happened to me. I learned there can be very serious consequences for my behavior. I learned that my work affects my witness. I learned that no matter what I am doing, whether I am cleaning a kennel or preaching a sermon, it is to be done as though it is for the Lord Himself. I also learned that there is no good reason to ever brush out a cat.

It was a hard lesson, but a necessary one.

✈☙❧

Prayer: "Thank You, Lord, that You have used failure in my life to teach me a lesson and to build my character."

Action: Sit down with your child who has suffered a failure recently and talk to him about what the Lord was teaching through it.

Good news is 'gooder' than the bad news

"...while we were still sinners, Christ died for us."
Romans 5:8

One of my favorite books from childhood was the story of "The Five Chinese Brothers."

Each brother had a special ability. The first brother was able to hold all the water of the sea in his mouth. One day he sucked up the sea to pick up fish off the bottom.

A boy came out into the empty sea and started making faces at the first brother, who couldn't hold the sea for long and tried to warn the boy before it spilled out. But the boy got caught up in the water and drowned.

The townsfolk arrested the first brother for the murder of the little boy and sentenced him to death. Before the execution, the second brother, whose neck was as strong as iron, took his brother's place. When the executioner tried to cut off his head, the sword bounced off.

The next night the third brother, whose legs could stretch, replaced the second. So when they threw him into the sea, he stretched his legs. His feet went down and his head stayed up.

They decided to burn him, so the fourth brother, who could not be burned, replaced the third.

Finally, the judge decided to suffocate the boy. But the fifth brother, who could hold his breath indefinitely, replaced the fourth.

In the end, the judge decided the boy must really be innocent and he let him go.

Well, I have good news and I have bad news. The bad news is that the story is not true. None of us is innocent and each of us one day must die. The statistic is pretty secure: One out of one dies.

In fact, the news is worse. The Bible tells us that we are already spiritually dead in trespasses and sins. I wonder ... when did that happen?

Did I die in my sins when I was 12 and had really honed rebellion to a fine art? That's when I remember throwing a dodge ball at Mrs. Beck, my sixth-grade teacher, on purpose, when she wasn't looking, and hitting her in the head.

But I died long before that. Was it when I was in the fourth grade? That's when I remember getting my mouth washed out with soap one Sunday because of something I had said at church, out loud, to a girl.

No, I died long before then. Was it when I was 5 and my mother told me to stay out of the poison oak, and I grabbed a handful of the healthiest poison oak I could find and rubbed it on my face? Was that when I died?

No, even before that. The Bible says that I was "brought forth in iniquity, and in sin my mother conceived me." I was born spiritually dead, and so were you. That's the bad news and it's really bad.

Do you want to hear the good news? The good news is even gooder than the bad news is bad. Gooder is better than badder! I know that is terrible grammar, but it is wonderful theology.

Jesus Christ came to take my place, and yours, and to die for our sins. And for a Christian, the story of the Chinese brothers does have a ring of truth. In Christ, there is nothing the world can do to me. They can take my physical life, but the life I have in Christ will never end.

In my sins, I could not live. In Christ, I cannot die. That is really good news!

✖❀✖

Prayer: "Lord, thank You for raising me from the spiritual death I born into and giving me new life in Christ!"

Action: Talk to your children about the pervasive worldview that says man is naturally good and it is his environment that makes him do bad things. Explain the biblical worldview that contradicts that.

First impressions are often wrong

"Do not set your mind on high things,
but associate with the humble.
Do not be wise in your own opinion."
(Romans 12:16)

The lady in the airline terminal had bought a book to read and a package of cookies to eat. The flight was twenty minutes from boarding, so she settled into her seat and began to read to pass the time. A few minutes into the first chapter, she was shocked by what was happening beside her. The man two seats over was fumbling to open the package of cookies in the seat between them. She couldn't believe it.

Who did this man think he was?

A perfect stranger was eating her cookies. Well! I am not going to just sit here and let him eat them all. So she reached over and took a cookie, biting into it with emphasis while stealing a glance at the man out of the corner of her eye as if to say, There! Take that! The man did not return her glance but kept reading his paper while reaching for another cookie. She waited a second, took another one and bit more loudly. He ignored her and took two this time. She ate another, and when they were down to the last cookie, the man broke it in half, got up and walked away. The lady could not fathom the nerve of this man, but soon the boarding call was made and she got on the plane. Still wondering about what planet this man could possibly have come from, she reached into her purse to find a tissue. That's when she found her package of cookies, still unopened.

It's true that you only get one chance to make a first impression. But it is also true that first impressions are often wrong. Stephen Covey, in "The 7 Habits of Highly Effective People," wrote of a mistake he made on a Sunday morning subway ride in New York:

People were sitting quietly — some reading newspapers, some lost in thought, some resting with their eyes closed. It was a calm, peaceful scene.

Then suddenly, a man and his children entered the subway car. The children were so loud and rambunctious that instantly the whole climate changed.

The man sat down next to me and closed his eyes, apparently oblivious to the situation. The children were yelling back and forth, throwing things, even grabbing people's papers. It was very disturbing. And yet, the man sitting next to me did nothing.

It was difficult not to feel irritated. I could not believe that he could be so insensitive as to let his children run wild like that and do nothing about it, taking no responsibility at all. It was easy to see that everyone else on the subway felt irritated, too. So finally, with what I felt was unusual patience and restraint, I turned to him and said, "Sir, your children are really disturbing a lot of people. I wonder if you couldn't control them a little more?"

The man lifted his gaze as if to come to a consciousness of the situation for the first time and said softly, "Oh, you're right. I guess I should do something about it. We just came from the hospital where their mother died about an hour ago. I don't know what to think, and I guess they don't know how to handle it either."

"Do not be wise in your own opinion." How many of us, me included, could avoid hurting someone with our words if we would first learn all of the information before we make a judgment? After all, our first impression is often wrong.

❦

Prayer: "Lord, please forgive me for the many times I have judged someone solely on outward appearance. Teach me to look with Your eyes at everyone I meet."

Action: Talk with your children about judging people based on their appearance and about labeling people according to their weakness, physical 'imperfection' or some other non-flattering distinguishing feature.

We are not called to the bench

*"We are hard pressed on every side, yet not crushed;
we are perplexed, but not in despair
(2 Corinthians 4:8)."*

When I was 13 years old, and weighed about 95 pounds, I joined my junior high school football team.

At one of the first practices where contact was involved, we got introduced to what the coach called "the meat grinder."

The name fit. Two boys lined up facing each other, 10 yards apart. On either side were tackling dummies, laid end to end, to create a narrow channel within which the "meat" could be ground. One boy was designated the runner, and handed a football. The other boy was designated the tackler, and was given jeers and whistles and other forms of "encouragement" by the rest of the team.

I was called into the meat grinder, and the coach gave me the ball. A 14-year-old named "C.D." (who as I recall was already shaving, stood 6 feet tall and weighed in at 165 lbs.) crouched on the other end, ready to grind me into powder.

If this were a Disney movie, I would have bowled C.D. over, knocking him senseless, and the other boys would have carried me on their shoulders to the locker room, coach running to catch us, anxious to talk to me about being their star running back that year.

This was not a Disney movie.

C.D. hit me like a freight train, driving me back past the point where I had started running, and finished the job by landing with his full weight on my skinny frame.

I lay there for a few minutes as the team snickered into their hands, and then I slowly raised my body from the dust, mentally checking to see if I still had all of my body parts.

The only thing I can figure is, the coach was trying to get me to quit, but I was too stupid or too proud or both.

I stayed on the team ... but not really.

You see, though our team went undefeated that year, I never saw one minute of playing time.

It wasn't because the coach didn't try to get me in the game. We would be up by 45 points at halftime, usually, and in the second half the coach would start putting in the scrubs. Eventually he made his way to me.

"Fox, have you been in the game yet?" he would always ask.

"Yes sir!" I would always squeak, mortified that he would call my bluff and make me play. The coach knew what was going on, and didn't push it.

I was a part of a championship team, but I never got in the game. I was on the sidelines the whole year, cheering on my team-mates, thankful to be there, but praying I would not have to actually go on the field and face my opponents.

The Apostle Paul said, "We are hard pressed on every side, yet not crushed; we are perplexed, but not in despair (2 Corinthians 4:8)."

Maybe Paul knew something about being in "the meat grinder." His response, unlike mine, was never to retreat to the bench and the protection of the sideline. Paul, like his Savior, ran toward difficulty, knowing that victory would come to those who put their trust in God.

I have been through a few "meat grinders" since that year in junior high. Not on the football field, but in the ministry, in mar-

There were also stations set up that offered beer to the runners. Or, Krispy Kreme doughnuts!

I did a double-take when Micah told me this. Why would someone running a 10-mile race even think about drinking a beer or slamming down a doughnut or two along the way? Why would anyone even offer such a thing to runners?

These competitors had been training for months, saying "no" to anything that would slow them down a fraction of a second. They had been disciplining their bodies, training hard, muscles and lungs burning, so that on race day they could ... eat a doughnut?

It made no sense. But when Micah explained the party atmosphere, the number of people who were "in the race" but not really competing to win, I understood.

It is the same way in the race of faith. There are some running the race of life with purpose and resolve, but many more who are cruising, skipping, or limping along. For either runner, there are many distractions along the way, many "offers" that will slow the steps, many temptations that will taste so good and right for a moment, but will bring a runner down to defeat at the end.

How many of my friends in the ministry have stumbled into sexual sin because they took their eyes off the goal just for a second? They were running along just fine, keeping in step with what the Lord had called them to and equipped them for, but then it happened. Just ahead, a table was set with everything they had a taste for but had said no to all their lives.

The thought came in a flash. "Hey, slow down a little and enjoy yourself. After all, you have earned it. You have worked hard, kept your nose clean all these miles. What will it hurt to take one little sip of pleasure. Everybody else is stopping, aren't they?"

But for the grace of God, there go I. That's why I keep reminding myself of the goal and the prize and the One who ran the race before me.

᯽

Prayer: "Lord, show me those little compromises I have taken that now hang on me like weights. Help me to be free to run Your race!"

Action: Throw off the weights the Lord shows you; write down the date that He showed you and what exactly each 'weight' is, and commit to keeping those weights off, by His grace!

I need friends who will tell me the truth!

"Faithful are the wounds of a friend,
but the kisses of an enemy are deceitful"
(Proverbs 27:6).

"Hey, Fox! What are you readin'?"

I knew that voice. It was coming from two seats behind me in history class. It belonged to a kid in our high school that everyone avoided because he was considered a nerd, a geek, a loser. I slowly turned, my mind spinning with anticipation of what I was about to do. My eyes fixed on my opponent. Actually, he wasn't trying to pick a fight; Rick was just asking an innocent question, but in that nerdish way of his that provoked so many in the school to tease him.

"Why don't you see for yourself?" I said, as I hurled the paperback I was reading. The missile found its desired target: Rick's pimply face. The same face that was red with acne now turned beet red with rage.

Rick stood up beside his desk, his overlarge Adam's apple moving up and down like a yo-yo, in sync with his breaths. He was angry and embarrassed by my attack. In all of the wisdom that I could muster as a tender young scholar of 17, I leaped to my feet and began to shadow box in front of Rick.

"You want a piece of me, Rick?" I taunted. "You want some of this?" I punched at him playfully, my fists pulling up just inches short of his face.

Rick was tall and as skinny as a toothpick, but his reach was at least a foot longer than mine. While I was floating like a butterfly, he decided to sting like a bee. Rick sent one true jab right to the center of my face. It was a direct hit to the mouth, exactly where I deserved it, and the fight was over just that quick. I was stunned as I reached up to my two front teeth and found they were not hanging out in their usual location.

You see, I had just gotten my braces off about a week earlier. Rick had undone in one second what my orthodontist (and my Dad's wallet, bless his soul) had taken 2 and 1/2 years to accomplish.

Not only that, but I was immediately sent to the principal's office, paddled, and sent home for three days' suspension for fighting in class. Talk about adding insult to injury!

Two root canals, two crowns, and thousands of dollars later, I was talking to my grandmother about the incident. I will never forget her counsel that day.

"Mark, you don't know anything about that boy. For all you know, his father beats him every day when he gets home from work. For all you know, that boy cries himself to sleep every night because of the suffering that you know nothing about. What that boy needs is a friend, and you just piled on to his misery. You got what you deserved."

My grandmother loved me enough to tell me the truth. She was a true friend in every sense of that word, faithful to 'wound' me rather than 'kiss' me. Even though her words hurt just about as much as Rick's punch to the kisser, my grandmother's counsel that day turned my anger to repentance, and my thoughts of revenge to remorse.

I need all the friends like that I can find.

❧❧❧

Prayer: "Thank You, Lord, that You have put friends in my life who are willing to speak the truth in love to me when I need it. Help me always to listen."

Action: Take a good friend out for lunch this week and thank him for having the courage to tell you the truth, even when it hurts.

Lay hold of the love of Christ

*"...that you, being rooted and grounded in love,
may be able to comprehend..."
(Ephesians 3:18-19)*

A while back, I decided to try running a longer distance than I had ever done before. It was nowhere near a marathon, like some of you have done. But it felt like a marathon. I was OK the first half, and for most of the way back. But with about 2 miles to go, I wanted to quit so badly I could almost taste it. My lungs were fine and my legs weren't that tired, but I was immersed in a colossal battle nonetheless. It was early in the morning, before folks were out working in their yards. If someone had been outside as I ran past, he might have wondered why this guy was shuffling along, saying, "Help me, Jesus ... Oh Lord, please, help me." When I wasn't praying for help, I was trying to encourage myself with things like, "Come on, Mark, don't quit. You can make it. Don't quit." I thought about what Jeff, a man in our church who competes in Iron Man Triathlons, had said at a recent Men's Breakfast: "You can do a lot more than you think you can." So, I kept running. I began to tell myself that I could run a half mile more before quitting. Then after that half mile, I would tell myself that I had at least one more half mile in me, and that I could do more than I thought I could.

But what I was really thinking about to the point that it became an obsession the last 2 miles ... was the finish line, and the water bottle that awaited me there. I had placed a bottle of water and a towel at the top of my driveway. The scene replayed in my mind over and over: I saw myself finishing the race, and grabbing the water bottle. I tried to decide how much I would pour on my head and how much I would pour in my mouth. I wondered how good it would feel to not be running any more. I wondered if I would ever stop running. I wondered if I was still going in the right direction.

I think I was delirious.

When I finished the race, and held that coveted prize of 16 ounces of the best-tasting water I have ever put in my mouth, it was a sweet reward.

How much sweeter and how much more satisfying is the love of Christ.

In Ephesians, Paul said that he prayed for us that we would be able to "comprehend ... the width and length and depth and height ... (of) the love of Christ." The word he used for comprehend in the Greek means to lay hold of something and make it your own. It means "to take" or "to seize," as a drowning man would grab a rope that is thrown overboard to him. As much as my body craved that liquid refreshment when I was feeling dehydrated from a long run, my soul thirsts much more for a love that will never end. The Bible teaches that such a love is there for the taking. Not only that, but the love of Christ is "wide:" it reaches to the whole world. There is no tongue or tribe or race or nation that is not included in his love. The love of Christ is as long as eternity. The love of Christ is deep enough to overcome the darkest sin. The love of Christ is so high that you and I will never get over it.

That's a prize worth running after.

୬ஃஃ৯

Prayer: "Lord, build my physical and my spiritual stamina as I run for the prize of the upward call of God in Christ Jesus."

Action: If you haven't already done so, start a physical exercise program. Remember, one of the ways we 'love our wives like Christ loved the church' is by taking care of our bodies so we can be around a long time, Lord willing!

Friend in need really is a friend, indeed

"A friend loves at all times, and a brother is born for adversity (Proverbs 17:17)."

"Preacher Fox!" The shrill voice on the other end of the phone belonged to Mrs. Johnson, an elderly widow who lived across the street. "Well, good morning, Mrs. Johnson. How are you?" "I'd be a lot better if my TV would work right. Could you come over and see what's wrong?" "Was it working last night?" I asked. "Yes. Can you come over and fix it, Mark?" she pleaded. "Yes, ma'am, I will in just a few minutes." "Are you coming right now?" she persisted. I had an office in my house in those days, on the second floor. From there, I had a clear view of the front porch of Mrs. Johnson's house. Which meant that she had a clear view of my office.

"You were up late last night," Mrs. Johnson said when I arrived. Her eyes were dancing but she was trying her best to make her face show "innocent concern." It wasn't working.

"Now, Mrs. Johnson," I chided, "how would you know that, unless you were spying on me?"

"I wasn't spying!" she replied, and pretended to be hurt, shooting her bottom lip out.

"OK," I said, "You were just 'concerned' that I wasn't getting my rest. Right?"

She smiled.

I said, "So let's take a look at that TV. I would not want you to miss one minute of your 'stories' this afternoon."

Mrs. Johnson led the way into the little den, where her console TV sat like a sentry. The room was cozy and warmed by a portable heater that hummed on the floor beside the sofa. The only other piece of furniture was a small coffee table, which is where I found the remote. I pointed and clicked. Nothing.

She was right. It would not turn on. Neither the remote nor the switch on the TV worked, so I pulled the set away from the wall and immediately found the problem.

"Mrs. Johnson, the TV is …" I started to say.

But when I turned around to tell her what I found, Mrs. Johnson was not in the den anymore. She was whistling a tune in the kitchen, fixing each of us a glass of Coke.

"Can you sit down and have some Coke with me?" she said, pointing to a chair at the table as I entered.

"Mrs. Johnson," I began as I sat down at the table, "your TV was unplugged."

"It was?" she replied, trying her best to look surprised.

"Yes, ma'am, it was. You don't know how that could have happened, do you?"

Mrs. Johnson lived alone with her toy poodle, "Precious." There was no one there but Mrs. Johnson who could have moved the TV set and pulled the plug.

She smiled and started to tell me all about her last trip to town, her dog's latest adventures, her family, and on and on. That's what she needed most that day, a friend. I guess I did, too.

⋖⋗

Prayer: "Lord, help me to love the ones who are lonely by giving them what they want and need the most—some of my time."

Action: If there is a widow in your church or in your neighborhood, get the kids and go over for a visit this week. See if there is anything you can do to help her around the house.

You can run, but you can't hide

"...and be sure your sin will find you out."
(Numbers 32:23)

I learned pretty early on in my Christian walk that I could run from God but I could not hide. Like the time I decided to skip church one Wednesday night and watch television at my grandparent's house. The only problem was, I really needed to have my glasses if I was going to watch TV, but I left them at home when I made the 2-mile drive over to Grandma's. Why? Do you really have to ask why a 17-year-old who wears Coke-bottle glasses because he's blind as a bat would leave them at home when he's driving through the neighborhood in the daytime? Have you forgotten how important it was to be cool when you were a teenager? It was important to me, too. And since I didn't have a chance at being cool, I had to at least look cool! That didn't work for me either, but I took comfort in the theory that since I couldn't see what I looked like without my glasses, maybe nobody else could either.

I headed home to collect my glasses. I slowed down just a little at the stop sign that was there just to test my skills at crossing from Grandma's road to our road without having to tap the brakes more than once. Driving along, singing a song, and then I saw it. A blur of blue in my rear view. I couldn't really tell what it was exactly, but I figured it wasn't the northern lights, so I pulled over. A few seconds later, a sheriff's deputy appeared at my door and I began to shake. I looked up and saw that his mouth was moving but

I couldn't hear what he was saying. My window! I rolled it down quickly and he said something again, but my ears had temporarily stopped working. He said it a third time, forcefully: "Get out of the car, sir!" I got out, half expecting him to slap some cuffs on me and drag me off to jail, since I had just had a wreck a few weeks earlier, a wreck that was my fault.

The sheriff's deputy was asking me another question, and I didn't answer because, once again, my head was ringing and my ears were refusing to work. The officer was beginning to think I was mute. And maybe blind. My glasses! He was asking about my glasses and why I wasn't wearing them, and according to my license I was required by law to wear them. Did I know that I had run a stop sign back there, and did I know that I could be cited for driving without my glasses, and did I know that I had nearly run a car off the road? And suddenly I was in a time warp, and my first-grade teacher was saying, "Mark, did you *know* that it was wrong to hit Kip in the head?"

I was finally able to speak and the sheriff's deputy kindly served God's purposes by giving me a ticket. I said "Yes, sir," as he explained the consequences of my actions, and I said "Yes, sir," as the DMV revoked my license for 60 days, and I said, "Yes, sir" as I paid my fine for running a red light.

The Bible says, "Your sin will find you out." That's for sure. I am thankful that the God who owns the universe governs my life. I can try to run from Him, but I can never hide. He loves me too much to let me do that.

❧❧

Prayer: "Thank You, Lord, that you don't let me get away with anything, because You love me and are committed to forming me into the image of Your Son!"

Action: Remind your children that one of the tactics of Satan is to convince young people that there are some things "that you just don't need to tell your parents." Encourage them to be completely honest and open about every area of their lives!

Are We Doing it For You, Daddy?

"...A time to keep silence, and a time to speak..."
(Ecclesiastes 3:7b)

It was suppertime at the Fox's, and we were discussing the Right to Life vigil that would be held that evening around the county courthouse. This was another anniversary of Roe v. Wade, the 1973 Supreme Court decision which legalized abortion in the United States.

One of the kids said to Judah, who was not sure about this vigil idea, "It's cool, Judah! You get to hold a candle!" Another added, "And we might get our picture in the paper!" Judah was mildly impressed, but I was surprised at what I heard from my children. I responded, "Guys! The reason we do this every year is not to hold candles or because we might get our picture in the paper. If that's why you're doing it, I'd rather you stay home."

There was a slight pause, and the older children looked intently at their broccoli. My problem is that even when I say the right thing (which happens every now and then), I still have a tendency to say it the wrong way! Thankfully, this evening was saved by my 5 year old who was not offended by my brusqueness. Judah flashed his big brown eyes at me and asked, "Are we doing it for you, Daddy?"

Cindy said, "Oh, how sweet," and my eyes pooled with tears at Judah's innocence. And I thanked God for the high and holy privilege He has given us as parents, the privilege and the delight of leading children to faith and obedience.

The question Judah asked made me think about my own motives for standing at the courthouse on the anniversary of Roe v. Wade. My heart whispered in prayer, "Am I doing it for You, Daddy?" Am I going to the courthouse to set an example for my children, so that they will see that the issue of the sanctity of life is more important than my temporary inconvenience? That is a good motive, but not the best. Am I going to the courthouse for the nearly 45 million babies who have been aborted since 1973? To pray and work, as Job said, for "the one who had no helper?" (Job 29:12). That is a good reason to go the vigil, I decided, but not the best. Judah's question rang in my heart: "Are we doing it for you, Daddy?"

That's really the issue for me. So I plan to take my family whenever possible to the courthouse, because my Father is passionate for life, and I am His child. I will add my little voice to the millions who are standing and praying and holding candles across the nation, hoping that the holocaust of abortion will end in our lifetime, because I believe God would have me do so. Is it a simple issue? No. I know the issue of abortion is volatile, with strong emotions on both sides. It can divide political parties and raise blood pressure and motivate voters and inspire poetry and song. Most life and death issues can.

I remember the day we lost our second born to miscarriage. The doctor explained, "We'll never know what happened. But there was something wrong with the embryo and God decided to end its life in the first trimester." Cindy and I wept for the son or daughter that we would not get to raise, but were comforted by the assurance that our Father is in control. He is the One who gives life, and takes life; He is the One who *is* life, and that's why I go to the courthouse. I am doing it for Daddy.

⋘⋙

Prayer: "Lord, help me to be a voice for those who cannot speak for themselves."

Action: Talk with your children about the wicked practice of abortion and make plans to participate with your local Right to Life organization in their next event.

Isn't it time to get back in?

"I write so that you may know how to conduct yourself
in the house of God, which is the church of the living God,
the pillar and ground of the truth."
(1 Timothy 3:15)

J. Wilbur Chapman used to tell the story of a man who stood up in one of his revival meetings and said, "I got off at the Pennsylvania depot as a tramp, and for a year I begged on the streets for a living. One day I touched a man on the shoulder and said, 'Hey mister, can you give me a dime?' As soon as I saw his face I was shocked to see that it was my own father. I said, 'Father, Father, do you know me?' Throwing his arms around me and with tears in his eyes, he said, 'Oh my son, at last I've found you! I've found you. You want a dime? Everything I have is yours.' Think of it. I was a tramp. I stood begging my own father for ten cents, when for 18 years he had been looking for me to give me all that he had."

Paul prayed for the church in Ephesus that they would be "filled with all the fullness of God." May I suggest to you today that the fullness of God can only be experienced in the context of the body of Christ? The fullness of God is in Christ, and the church is Christ's body. So if you are unsatisfied with your experience of who God is, it may be because you are not walking with other believers in a healthy, biblical church. Or, maybe one of the following scenarios describes your current position better.

It may be because you are sitting on the side of the pool with just your toes in the water. It may even be that you are sitting on the back of the wagon, if you will allow me that old-time picture, looking back and even complaining about times gone by. Not only that, you may be dragging your feet as the wagon moves along, impeding the progress of the wagon. It is sad that though the gates of hell can not stand against the church, disobedient believers sure can! Paul didn't have to write any letters to churches that were having problems overcoming hell. He wrote letters to churches that were being defeated and distressed by people in bondage to sin, people in bondage to false teaching, people in bondage to a life committed to self-fulfillment.

If you are not experiencing the fullness of God in the body of Christ, then may I suggest you do one of two things as soon as you can. First, if you identify with the pool analogy, the fix is simple. Take the plunge! But before you do that, repent. Ask the Lord to forgive you for wasting time on the side of the pool. Also, renew your mind. You are not sitting on the side of the pool for no reason at all. Ask the Lord to show you what scared you out of the water, and I know very well that the church can be a difficult place with lots of problems. Believe me, I know. Not just from experience with people who have problems but from experience with my own problems and sins and shortcomings!

If you are not experiencing the fullness of God because you are sitting on the back of the wagon, dragging your feet, then do two things quickly. First, repent! Then, get off the tailgate of the wagon and climb in facing the right direction. You will be amazed at the new perspective. You will be welcomed by the other passengers. You will be blessed with the fullness of God in His church.

❧

Prayer: "Lord, help me to give of myself to Your work and to serve our local church through the stewardship of my tithes and talents."

Action: Be faithful to the fellowship of believers through attendance, service, giving, and prayer. Ask the pastor if there are ways your family could serve the church.

God dwells in heaven, hearts

"in everything give thanks;
for this is the will of God in Christ Jesus for you."
(2 Thessalonians 5:18)

I don't even remember what Cindy and I were fighting about now. But I remember what happened to end the fight. It was about 5 years ago, in the fall of the year. Jesse was nine then and he had already had three "febrile seizures," where his fever spiked and he went into convulsions. His first one was when he was 18 months old, and it happened right after church on a Wednesday night, in our kitchen. The next two happened during a Sunday morning service. Seriously! He stopped those meetings cold, at least until we got things under control. This last one happened at home again. I put Jesse in an ice bath to try to get his fever down but he would not come out of the convulsion, so I called 911 and the first responders got there quickly. After we had been at the hospital for a few hours, two grateful parents took their nine-year-old home and thanked God that everything was fine.

We could not relate any more to the anger we had felt towards each other in the hours before the seizure occurred. It just didn't matter. I remember a sweet hug and a "Will you forgive me?" spoken almost in unison.

As we stand on the threshold of another day of giving thanks for our many blessings, may I remind you that most of what you are upset about right now, in the grand scheme of things, just does not matter? Use the "four-year rule" from my story as an example. Four years from now, will you even remember what you were fuming about? Hey, if you have my memory, you can use the 4-day rule! Either way, whatever has your shorts in a wad right now will be long gone in mere days or months and it just won't matter. Then you will be stuck with having to maintain your anger just as a "matter of principle," or do the mature thing and put it away for good.

Gratitude should be a powerful motivator. That's why Jesus asked, when only one of 10 lepers he healed came back to say thank you, "Were there not 10 cleansed? But where are the nine?"

Robert Capon wrote, "A person who is 'well enough to enjoy the blessings' expresses gratitude to the source from which it comes. There were 10 requests for mercy and healing and only one who returned to express their gratitude. While the other nine lepers may have been grateful, only one returned to say "thank you."

Why not try this experiment? Send a note of thanks to 10 people this week who have influenced you, blessed you and been an encouragement to you. But don't limit that list of ten to friends and loved ones. Send a few notes also to people from whom you have become estranged, people who have hurt or disappointed you in some way, people that you might even consider to be your 'enemies.' Be careful not to bring up past offenses. Just be grateful and express that as simply and as honestly as you can. You never know what God might do with such an act of humility.

I like being around people who have grateful hearts. It reminds me of what my own heart should look like. Someone once said that God has two dwelling places. One is in heaven and the other is the thankful heart.

❦

Prayer: "Lord, help me to put away any grudges and please pull out any roots of bitterness in my life."

Action: Send those letters this week!

Our Hope is In the Lord

"He heals the brokenhearted and binds up their wounds."
(Psalm 147:3)

A young man in our church was nearly 12 years old when he fell out of a tree in his backyard and broke his leg. When the doctors prepared to do surgery on Micah, they discovered that he had leukemia. Micah's battle with the deadly cancer continued for four years. He had a bone marrow transplant at Duke Hospital. One of his sisters (Micah was the third-born of nine children) was a perfect match with her bone marrow, so hopes were high that this would be a cure. But not long after the transplant, the leukemia came roaring back, meaner than ever. The doctors at Baptist Hospital tried a stronger chemotherapy to bring Micah into remission so that a second bone marrow transplant could be attempted. But the leukemia did not budge, and the doctors told the family there was nothing else they can do.

Micah went home from the hospital and Hospice was called in.

But Micah was in no way giving up hope. When the first bone marrow transplant failed and the powerful drugs did not work, Micah said to his father, "This means that either God is going to heal me or take me home to be with Jesus." Once when I visited him in the hospital, I said, "Micah, what are you asking the Lord to do for you?" He replied, "His will." Then he flashed that shy smile that was Micah's trademark.

He didn't want to talk about himself. He would much rather talk about his passion, which was playing and singing worship music. I wish all of you could have heard Micah play his guitar and sing at the top of his lungs about the Savior he loved so much. On a Friday night, one of his last at Baptist Hospital, two families came to visit Micah and ended up playing guitars and singing with Micah for two hours. It was the talk of the hospital. The nurse that stopped in to check on Micah lingered longer than usual. Another nurse said later, "That sounded like angels' singing." Who knows? Maybe there was a heavenly chorus joining in.

A few weeks before he died, I asked Micah if there was a particular passage of Scripture that meant a lot to him. He quoted Psalm 147:3: "He heals the brokenhearted and binds up their wounds." Micah knew that God was going to heal him completely. He knew that God would either heal him from leukemia through a miracle, or God would heal him from leukemia through death. Either way, his hope was in the Lord to do what was best.

"Micah," I continued, "do you have any fear about what might happen?"

He shook his head, "No."

"Are you at peace, then?" I asked. Again, Micah gave me that shy smile and said, "Yes."

God gave Micah and his family His amazing grace to walk through this valley for four years, and to hold onto the Lord all the way through. During the last days, at the memorial service, and to this day, the family continues to give God the glory and tell all who will hear about Micah's battle and his ultimate victory. Micah's father would stand up often in church and say, "Our hope is in the Lord." It is the best place for hope.

◦❀◦

Prayer: "Lord, thank you for Your promise that You will never leave or forsake us, even when we walk through the dark valley of disease and death. Be my only hope, Lord!"

Action: Is there someone in your church or family who is walking through such a valley right now? Have your family send them a card with encouragement from each one of you.

I thank God for the Pilgrims

"Do not remove the ancient landmark
which your fathers have set."
(Proverbs 22:28)

Call me politically incorrect if you like, but I tend to believe the history books that were written before the 1950s more than the ones that are written today. For one thing, the older history books tell us that the Pilgrims had their first Thanksgiving celebration to give thanks to ... God!

Dr. Paul Vitz, a professor of psychology at New York University, has studied the bias against religious references in public school texts. He reported, for example, the second grade text by Riverside (formerly Rand McNally) has 31 pages on the Pilgrims, but it describes them entirely without reference to religion.

Vitz told the story of one mother in an upper middleclass New York City suburb who complained to the principal when her first grade son was told by his teacher that at Thanksgiving the Pilgrims gave thanks to the Indians. The mother told the principal that it was simply a historical fact that Thanksgiving was a time when the Pilgrims gave thanks to God, but the principal replied that the mother's position "was just opinion and not documented fact," and therefore the school could not teach it. The principal said that "they could only teach what was contained in the history books." ("Public School Textbooks and Christian Values," by Wayne Grudem)

This is what is documented as having been written by William Bradford, governor of the Plymouth Colony, as a proclamation.

"... I, your magistrate, do proclaim that all ye Pilgrims, with your wives and little ones, do gather at ye meeting house, on ye hill, between the hours of 9 and 12 in the day time, on Thursday, November ye 29th of the year of our Lord one thousand six hundred and twenty-three, and the third year since ye Pilgrims landed on ye Pilgrim Rock, there to listen to ye pastor, and render thanksgiving to ye Almighty God for all His blessings."

Thanksgiving is a time, as the Bible says, to "Give thanks to the Lord! Call upon his name; make known his deeds among the peoples." With that in mind, I offer this meager effort of my own at poetry as a reminder of the lessons God teaches us through the Pilgrims.

Men of courage and women of honor, Children wide-eyed with excitement, A journey of 65 days across the Atlantic, One crewman and one passenger lost, One baby, Oceanus, born, The Pilgrims landed and the new world was Forever changed. A brutal winter brought sickness and death, The spring came none too soon, And found the weary Pilgrims nearly cut in half, 46 were gone. The Wampanoag came in spring and taught The Pilgrims how to plant and fish and live, And God rekindled hope. With harvest time, the Pilgrims rejoiced, And asked their new friends to come and share, Massasoit and 90 of his people came And feasted for three days. The Governor led the Pilgrims in giving thanks To God for His providential care, And the colony bowed their heads. O God our help in ages past, We stand in debt to the Pilgrims, For their courage to come and their Faith to stay, For their Compact of laws that laid a Foundation, for their zeal to teach and reach The lost. We give thanks today, O Lord, And we commit our lives again to You. Though the path ahead may bring suffering or death, Give us Pilgrim courage and faith to stay In the Plymouth place where You have planted us, With hope that does not disappoint And love that never fails.

⚜

Prayer: "Lord, thank You that we stand on the shoulders of those who have gone before us and sacrificed for freedom. Let us not take that freedom for granted or squander it through careless living."

Action: Read a good book (not a politically correct one!) on the Pilgrims and discuss the origin of Thanksgiving with your children.

Teenagers should think, act like adults

"When I was a child, I spoke as a child...
but when I became a man, I put away childish things."
(1 Corinthians 13:11)

How many times have you heard commencement speakers say to college graduates, "Welcome to adulthood?" Or, "Now you are moving from childhood to adulthood?"

I believe there is something fundamentally flawed with the idea that teenagers should be expected and even taught that they should act and think and speak like children.

Jesus was 12 when he was brought to Jerusalem by his parents and participated with them in the Feast of the Passover as an adult. When they could not find him later as they traveled back to Nazareth, they were concerned. They hurried back to Jerusalem where they found their son in the temple, teaching the elders. Do you remember what Jesus said to his mother?

"Why did you seek me? Did you not know that I must be about my Father's business?" (Luke 2:48-49).

Though he went back to Nazareth and was subject to his parents, Jesus was not a child any longer. He had to be about His Father's business.

I believe that a child becomes a "young adult" at the age of 12 or 13.

Paul said that when he was a child, he spoke, understood, and thought as a child, "…but when I became a man, I put away childish things." Paul did not put away childish things and become an "adolescent." That is modern terminology that many use today to excuse the childish behavior of teenagers. Paul left childhood to become a man.

I saw a story a few years ago entitled "Kidults reluctant to leave the nest." This report used new words popular in the culture now such as "kidults" and "adultescents," and suggested the brain of a 17-year-old may not be as fully developed as a 30-yearold.

One sociologist remarked, "If someone insults you at work, an older teen is more likely to throw a punch where an adult would pause and make a sarcastic comment."

I have to confess, neither one of those responses to an insult at work sounds mature, but the reason the 17-year-old throws a punch may have less to do with his brain's maturity and more to do with what he has been told and taught since he was born.

The message teens hear most often today from school, media, psychology texts and even pulpits is, "You are a child and children behave childishly, and we can't expect you to be anything else."

But that's the wrong message. If the biblical message is that adulthood begins at 12 or 13, then what have we done to our young men and women by continuing to treat them like children, and allowing them to behave that way?

Voddie Baucham said this at a Uniting Church and Family Conference in April, 2005: "We have taken an army that God has given to the body and said, 'Lay down your arms and go play.'"

If Voddie is right, and I believe he is, then the implications for the church and the culture are enormous. We have stunted the growth of the next generation if we tell them they don't have to grow up until they move out.

We have handicapped the church if we treat these young warriors like they are bench-warmers who are not expected to "get in the game" until they get married or finish college.

❦

Prayer: "Lord, forgive me for the times I have treated my teens like they were still children. Help me to look at them with Your understanding and to challenge them to put away childish things."

Action: Have a talk with your teens about what it means to move from childhood into adulthood and pray with them as they make that move. You may want to have a special ceremony in which you welcome each 12 or 13 year old into the rank of adults!

Let the young ones grow up

*"Let no one despise your youth,
but be an example to the believers in word, in conduct,
in love, in spirit, in faith, in purity"
(1 Timothy 4:12).*

My family visited Boston a few years ago where we heard a young sailor aboard the USS Constitution tell us the ship's story. "Old Ironsides," as she was affectionately called, was a frigate in the US Navy, active before and during the War of 1812. She went undefeated in her short career, winning 33 battles and losing none. The key to her victories, perhaps, was the employment of "small boys" and "powder monkeys," as they were called. These were boys and young men, ages 9 to 17. The "small boys" were used to keep water flowing over the loose powder and the hot floor as the big guns were firing. If they were faithful in that task, a boy or young man could become a "powder monkey." These kept the big guns supplied with gunpowder, running below deck to get the powder, running back up to the guns to help load them. The sailor giving us the tour said the USS Constitution could fire 3 rounds in the time it took the British to fire 2, which helped assure our victory and the ship's longevity.

What if the Navy had said, "You boys run and play soldier with sticks and rocks. Come back when you are full-grown men!"

Isn't that what the church has said, in effect, to our young people? "Go play Xbox, immerse yourself in music and concerts and videos. Go hang out at the mall. Go dabble in the pleasures of the world. Come back when you get it out of your system and are old enough to serve the church."

Rather, we want to train and disciple young people in the Word, prayer, ministry and outreach. Here is a partial list of ways we give the teens (young adults) opportunities to serve the Lord and his church.

Young adults are encouraged to prepare to play and sing skillfully and present music for the Sunday morning services.

Young adults are encouraged to participate in the home group meetings by coming prepared with a testimony of how God is working in their lives that week.

Young adults are encouraged to discover and use their spiritual gifts to edify the body of Christ.

Young men are asked to help with meeting physical needs in the body (helping a family move, landscaping a yard for a family in the church, helping an elderly person in the church or community).

We have had a young man running the soundboard at church during the service for the past several years. When one got ready to leave for college, he trained another young man who was interested in learning.

My oldest son wanted to invest in the young men at the church, so he asked me about starting a weekly Bible Study for them. He did so, with the help of one of the elders.

Young ladies are called on regularly to assist Moms in the church with childcare or housecleaning or preparing to move.

Young people go regularly on short-term missions trips and share in the teaching and ministry.

Young people are encouraged in evangelism and given opportunities to reach the lost.

Paul wrote to young Timothy, "Let no one despise your youth, but be an example to the believers in word, in conduct, in love, in spirit, in faith, in purity" (1 Timothy 4:12). Paul knew the tendencies we in the church have, to push aside the young or worse to entertain them into mediocrity. I contend that we cannot afford to do that any longer. Let the young ones grow up.

❧❀❧

Prayer: "Thank You, Lord, that you have given me team members, my own children, to serve with me in the battle!"

Action: Encourage your church to move in this direction of allowing the teens to step into adult responsibilities, with training and encouragement, of course!

Going there with Daddy

"The Lord God (is) in your midst. The Mighty One will save;
He will rejoice over you with gladness,
He will quiet you with His love,
He will rejoice over you with singing."
(Zephaniah 3:17)

When I was growing up, there were two things that would ALWAYS get me out of bed in a hurry. I remember it like it was yesterday the family vacations that started at 0-dark-thirty, as we would roll out of bed and hit the road when it was still "a great while before dawn." Dad liked to drive when the roads were empty, and Mom liked to get her feet in the ocean as soon after sunup as possible, and we three boys didn't mind. We knew we would sleep all the way down wake up at the BEACH! Mom still tells the story about the time we stopped halfway to the beach at gas station, and I groggily jumped out of the car with my bucket and plastic shovel, looking for the sand. Boy was I disappointed that my nap was interrupted for a pit stop! But I crawled back into the car, confident that my father would get us there…

The other time of the year when I relished getting up long before the sun did was on Christmas morning. That was the day when something waited for me downstairs and it was always a surprise. I remember many of those nights, laying in my bed bug-eyed, staring at the ceiling, praying to God to let me go to sleep *now* so I could hurry and wake up in the morning! I would finally drift off to a fitful sleep, sometimes dreaming that I overslept and missed Christmas! I never did, and Dad and Mom always had something special for us under the tree, a surprise with our names on them...

Where am I going with these stories? Simply here: I still love Christmas morning, and I still love vacations with my family, especially to the beach, but I am not "limited" any longer to enjoying getting up early only two days a year. Our heavenly Father calls us out of bed early in the morning every day, just to be with Him. He whispers to us in the night that He loves us and can't wait to surprise us with His gifts that are new every morning. I confess that sometimes I sleep right through that opportunity, but not because I don't want to be in His presence. Sometimes my own busy-ness crowds out the most important business: a relationship with the God who created me for Himself. He loves us and delights in us, His creation. The Bible says it like this:

When I think about the God who created the universe out of nothing, speaking the worlds into existence, flinging the stars into space, making the galaxies appear with a single word, I am awed by His unspeakable power and might. Then I am reminded that this same God came to earth in the flesh, took on the form of a servant, and suffered and died because His creation had rejected Him and gone our own way. I am awed by His ineffable love and mercy. This mighty, loving, gracious God calls me and you to meet with Him, to draw near to Him, to get to know Him, to see what surprises He has for us. That's what gets me out of bed in the morning. I know that no matter where this day may take me, I go there with Him...

❧❀❧

Prayer: "Lord, help me to get 'blanket-victory' and rise early to spend time with You every morning."

Action: Set your alarm thirty minutes earlier for tomorrow morning and make sure you get up when it goes off!

Jesus taught us downward mobility

"The Word became flesh and dwelt among us."
(John 1:14)

An ice storm in December 2002 that left much of North Carolina out of power for up to five days.

I will be honest with you. It was an adventure for a while, but then it got old, even for my children. And it was hard for me not to be jealous, maybe even a little bit ticked off, when I heard reports one after another from people whose power had been restored.

I remember driving into town on the fourth day, on my way to Elon University to take a shower in the locker room, hearing on the radio that Duke Power had restored more than 1.2 million of its customers who had lost power. The reporter said, "But there are still around 250,000 who are without power, mostly in Durham, Chapel Hill and Greensboro."

I yelled at the radio, "Not all of them! There's still a few of us insignificant little peons in Burlington!"

Now, given the choice, which would you choose? Power or no power? Water to flush your toilets or no water? OK, that's an easy one. We would almost always choose comfort over primitive living conditions. Let's increase the stakes a bit.

Let's say your boss calls you into his office this week and says, "I am offering you a promotion. It will mean more time at the office, more time out of town, and more time away from your family. But the pay raise and the perks are significant."

Would you take the promotion?

Let's say the boss says, further, "You can move up the third floor to a corner office. You will be away from the friends you work with now, but the view is amazing."

Would you take the move?

We will almost always choose more comfort than less, more space than less, more pay than less, more perks than less, more status than less.

We all live with an incredible pull towards upward mobility. And many believe that on the other side of that promotion or that upward climb will be satisfaction, even joy, peace, fulfillment, and security.

But what happens to many on their way up that ladder is that they begin to feel pretty good about themselves and their abilities; they begin to develop a distaste, even a disgust for those around them who "haven't yet made it."

They even get to the place where they don't see a need for that wife who helped get them there and they don't have time for the kids anymore (too much to do!). They start wondering why people around them are so slow and so immature and so ignorant ... get the picture?

The track of upward mobility is a dangerous one. Worst of all, the track of upward mobility can deceive one into thinking that the real meaning of life is found in status, success, and stuff. But Jesus said, "For what will it profit a man if he gains the whole world, and loses his own soul (Mark 8:36)?"

As we stand on the threshold of this Christmas season, keep in mind that Jesus taught and lived downward mobility. John 1:1 tells us that Jesus existed in the beginning with God, because Jesus is God. But Jesus did not stay in heaven. Love came down. John 1:14 says, "The Word became flesh and blood and moved into the neighborhood."

The great news of Christmas is that Jesus was "born that man no more may die." Love came down ... and that's worth celebrating.

Prayer: "Lord, help me to keep my 'status' and my 'stuff' in perspective and to live in light of the truth that You lived a 'downwardly mobile' life!

Action: Take your family (and others from the church, perhaps) to a modest nursing home in your community and spend time with the folks there, loving them giving them simple gifts they can use, singing Christmas carols to them.

This pageant had a twist

"For there is born to you this day in the city of David a Savior..."
(Luke 2:11)

One of my favorite Christmas stories took place in the '60s and was written about in the "Baptist Herald." Here's an edited version of Dina Donahue's "Trouble at the Inn."

For many years now, whenever Christmas pageants are talked about in a certain Midwest town, someone mentions the name of Wallace Purling.

Wally was 9 that year and in the second grade, though he should have been in the fourth. Most people in town knew that he had difficulty in keeping up. He was big and clumsy, slow in movement and mind. Still, his class, all of whom were smaller than he, had trouble hiding their irritation when Wally would ask to play ball with them, or any game in which winning was important. Most often they'd find a way to keep him out but Wally would hang around anyway, not sulking, just hoping. He was always a helpful boy, and the natural protector of the underdog. Sometimes if the older boys chased the younger ones away, Wally might say, "Can't they stay? They're no bother."

Wally fancied the idea of being a shepherd with a flute in the Christmas pageant that year, but the director, Miss Lumbar, assigned him to a more important role. After all, she reasoned, the Innkeeper did not have too many lines and Wally's size would make his refusal of lodging to Joseph more forceful. And so it happened that the usual large, partisan audience gathered for the town's yearly extravaganza of beards, crowns, halos and squeaky voices. No one on stage or off was more caught up in the magic of the night than Wallace Purling. He stood in the wings and watched the performance with such fascination that from time to time Miss Lumbar had to make sure he didn't wander on stage before his cue.

Then the time came when Joseph appeared, tenderly guiding Mary to the Inn's door. Wally the innkeeper was there, waiting.

"What do you want?" Wally said, swinging the door open roughly.

"We seek lodging."

"Seek it elsewhere," Wally looked straight ahead but spoke vigorously. "The Inn is filled."

"Sir, we have asked everywhere in vain. We have traveled far and are very weary."

"There is no room in this Inn for you." Wally looked properly stern.

"Please, good Innkeeper, this is my wife, Mary. She is heavy with child and needs a place to rest. Surely you must have some small corner for her. She is so tired."

Now, for the first time, the Innkeeper relaxed his stance and looked down at Mary. With that, there was a long pause, long enough to make the audience a bit tense with embarrassment.

"No! Be gone!" the prompter whispered from the wings.

"No!" Wally repeated automatically, "Be gone!"

Joseph sadly placed his arm around Mary and Mary laid her head upon her husband's shoulder and the two of them started to move away. The Innkeeper did not return inside his Inn, however. Wally stood there in the doorway, watching the forlorn couple. His mouth was open, his brow creased with concern, his eyes filling unmistakably with tears.

And suddenly this Christmas pageant was different from all the others.

"Don't go, Joseph," Wally called out. "Bring Mary back." Wally's face grew into a bright smile. "You can have my room!"

Some say that was the best Christmas pageant the town had ever seen, the year that Wally Purling opened his heart, and the Inn, to the one of whom the angel said, "there is born to you ... a Savior, who is Christ the Lord" (Luke 2:11). May we do the same.

❦

Prayer: "Thank You, Lord, that You made room in Your heart for me; may I do the same for You this Christmas, and every day for the rest of my life!"

Action: Gather the family on Christmas Eve and read the story of the birth of Christ from Matthew 1 and Luke 2. Ponder these things in your hearts.

These are a few of my favorite things

Sitting by the fire in the den, cozy and warm, reading the birth narrative from Luke 2 as a family. A new tradition will begin next year when we watch the DVD of "The Nativity Story," one of the best movies Hollywood has ever produced on the life of Christ.

Feeling the frost snip and snap at my fingers and nose as we stand in the front yard of a neighbor or church shut-in and sing Christmas carols. The home group that meets at our house will deliver a "blessing basket" to one of the elderly couples in the church and sing carols to them this year.

Trimming the Christmas tree, laughing at ornaments that have been around for years, and smiling at the memories others evoke.

Sipping hot chocolate, eating fudge that I made with the kids, and watching "It's a Wonderful Life" together with family and friends. The movie always reminds me of what this world would be like had Jesus not come to save us. It would make "Pottertown" look like Disneyworld.

Driving through neighborhoods and enjoying the variety of 'light shows,' from the sublime to the humorous. I appreciate the creativity and the trouble some go to in decorating their house and yard, while at the same time wonder if they know that the light of the world has come. No amount of incandescence can match his brilliance or his majesty. John wrote, "The light shines in the darkness, and the darkness did not overcome it."

Tapping my toes to the sounds of "Holiday Pops" as presented by the North Carolina Symphony Orchestra. I never knew until a few years ago that the "horse-whinny" sound at the end of "Sleigh-Ride" is made by a trumpet!

Sorting shoeboxes at Operation Christmas Child in Boone, helping to bless the lives of children somewhere far away. This year 43 of us from church were able to help send off part of the 8 million boxes stuffed with toys, candy, clothing and other goodies. Children in 95 countries will receive a Christmas gift and the story of the first Christmas in their own language.

Reading aloud through one of Arnold Ytreeide's advent stories such as "Bartholomew's Passage." We follow Bartholomew, a young Hebrew boy in Palestine just before Jesus' birth, as he tries to find his family and meets up with incredible adventures.

Stuffing seven stockings with my wife on Christmas Eve after all the children are sent off to bed. Some of my best memories of Christmas as a child are lying in bed on the night of December 24th, listening to my parents downstairs as they 'prepared' the treasures for the next morning.

Receiving Christmas cards from friends and family that we hear from only once a year, and from those we see every week and love more and more. I also love writing the "Fox News Report" (Motto: HE decides, we report! News about how God has worked in the Fox family this year) and sending it to family and friends all across the country.

Gathering with extended Fox and Lawson families and catching up on loved ones' lives.

Watching the dancing eyes of my children as they open their gifts and empty their stockings.

Celebrating the birth of Christ with the family at Antioch when the special songs and readings are offered as a gift to him.

These are just a few of my favorite memories of Christmases past and present. May God bless you and yours with his peace on earth and goodwill toward men this Christmas and always!

***

Prayer: "Lord, you are the greatest gift of all. When the presents are all unwrapped and the stockings are emptied, remind me again of Your gift of life that just gets sweeter each day!"

Action: As your family enjoys Christmas together, spend time going around the circle in prayer, thanking God for the many ways He has given to you this past year.

Afterword

I hope this book has been an encouragement to you. If so, you may want to read my other books, *Family-Integrated Church* and *Who's Afraid of Public Speaking*. The first book is the story of how God led our church from a traditional model to a family-integrated model. I tell lots of stories and cover topics as varied as qualifications for elders to music styles to having a missionary mindset as a church. You can find the book on Amazon.com or any number of other online booksellers' sites, or you can order a signed copy directly from me ($15, which includes shipping and handling). The book on Public Speaking is a handbook for effective speaking that was written with homeschooled teens in mind, but it has been bought and used by adults as well. The twenty lessons, complete with assignments, will take the reluctant speaker through the steps of researching, writing, and delivering a good speech. The book covers logic and persuasion, finding good illustrations, methods of organizing your speech, overcoming stagefright, and much more. You can order it directly from me ($17, which includes shipping and handling). This book has been recommended by Cathy Duffy (<u>Christian Home Educators Curriculum Manual</u>) and Debra Bell (Home School Resource Center). Send a check for $17 for the Public Speaking book, $15 for the Family-Integrated Church book, or $30 for both to:

J. Mark Fox, P.O. Box 40, Elon, NC 27244.

You may also sign up to receive my weekly newspaper columns via email. Just send an email to me at markfox@anti-ochchurch.cc, and let me know that you want to subscribe. The columns will be delivered to you weekly, free of charge, until you tell us to stop!

Finally, if you are ever in the Burlington area of North Carolina, please come and worship with us at Antioch Community Church. You will find us every Sunday at 10:00am at 1600 Powerline Rd., Elon, NC, 27244. Go to www.antiochchurch.cc for more information and for a map.

May the Lord bless you!

In Christ,

Mark

CPSIA information can be obtained
at www.ICGtesting.com
Printed in the USA
BVOW04s1240251116

468718BV00001B/38/P